ministering to kids
who don't fit

Mark A. Simone

ACCENT PUBLICATIONS
Colorado Springs, Colorado

ACCENT PUBLICATIONS

P.O.Box 36640
4050 Lee Vance View
Colorado Springs, Colorado 80936

Library of Congress Catalog Card Number 93-71657

ISBN 0-89636-296-5

Second Printing

Contents

Dedication

This book is dedicated to all of the wonderful people of my church in Ravenna, Ohio who served as the "laboratory" for this book. The members and friends of First Congregational loved the many kids who came through their doors with a love excelled only by Jesus.

More importantly, this book is dedicated to my wife, Kathy, who believed in this book when I had lost all hope and who challenged me to make this the best avenue of ministry it could possibly be. I love you, honey!

and in appreciation

Some very special people aided in making this book possible by sharing their information and insights. Thank yous to Ray Isackila, David Whaley, Judy Kramer, Matt Simone, Mary Nelson, Dr. Mary Ellen Drushal, Dr. Doug Little, Maureen "Buffy," Don Preslan, Daniel Simone, and the dozens of teenagers whose stories are reflected on these pages.

May God continue to bless you all as you use your special gifts to serve Him.

1/ Youth Groups — For All Teenagers

My first youth group consisted of six very nice, middle-class, normal, pretty and handsome, energetic junior high kids. We met in my home each week and we had a blast! The kids loved the program and began to find their places in the family of Christ. They invited their friends. Their friends began to invite others and in one year the six multiplied to a regular group of about 50 kids. Keep in mind, we are still meeting at my home, on my carpets and furniture, and near my refrigerator!

As the group became larger, it developed diversity. There were now kids with problems larger than anything I had ever experienced in my short, sheltered life. My parents had divorced when I was young, but so had everyone else's, or so it seemed. I could relate to the divorce issue. But what about the handicapped kids who came to youth group? Or the abused kids? Or the 14-year-old girl who had an abortion? And that boy who had the long delinquency record? Or the children of very messy divorces? Larger group. . . larger potential for some different life situations.

I wanted to keep these kids in the youth group. But I realized that I needed to make some changes to do so. Initially, my wife and I decided to keep the kids in our home. We sensed that the home environment was one of the main attractions for the kids.

Then an orange pop stain appeared on the carpet. No biggie, the carpet was old. The noise level was getting louder and louder, and we had two young children who needed to sleep. We managed that one, too, by starting the group earlier and sending them home right after. However, no amount of compensation could overcome the crisis when one young lady thought it would be funny to jump (literally jump!) onto the rockers of my wife's favorite antique rocking chair in the hopes of scaring her friend who was sitting in it. She jumped, landed solidly, and. . .snapped off one of the rockers without making the chair so much as teeter.

Other minor dramas occurred. Like missing food and kids walking in at all hours. Or kids coming by at supper time...every evening. Rougher problems also began to frequent our life, like unintentional abuse to our kids, difficult kids giving us trouble and frightening our children, and stolen property. Soon after, we unveiled the new youth room at the church!

Even with the new, more spacious room and the restored peace of mind at our home, I sensed that something still was not right. I couldn't deny the impending panic that was beginning to well up within me. In that first year I evaded the real issues that the group was facing.

I had blamed the problems on the size of my living room. Now, with the larger room in the church, I had to acknowledge that the problems were not caused by location, they were seeded within the group itself. No amount of success, like transforming six kids into an active group of 50 in about a year, could ease the incredible tensions I was finally allowing to surface. I was at a crisis point and I had no idea how to solve it.

In that first year we added to the group:

—a brother and sister whose parents were deaf.

—a person with serious physical problems.

—a person who was partially retarded.

—a person with sexual orientation problems.

—numerous juvenile delinquents.

—a young person with a genetically-based mental illness.

—lots of kids whose parents had divorced.

—many teenagers from poor families.

Notice that I have not mentioned one of the "normal" problems often associated with adolescence. All of the kids also had those. Many of them also had special-life situations and they literally made up the majority of the group.

I decided to investigate the available books on these topics at my local Christian bookstore. I was sure I could find something to solve my growing problem of helping these kids with special problems become a part of the youth group. But, nothing on the shelves helped me or my ministry. I felt like I was on my own from the human standpoint.

That incredibly stressful and frustrating time gave birth to this book. My hope is that others, volunteers or paid staff youth leaders, when faced with similar situations, can benefit from my discoveries and save their time for great activities and inspiring Bible studies.

Wise and healthy people do not have to learn everything by personal experience. There isn't enough time! Proverbs 22:3 tells us, "A prudent man sees danger and takes refuge, but the simple keep going and suffer for it." If we required first-hand experience with every difficulty, problem and sin that life has to offer in order to be fair and informed leaders, we wouldn't have the time or strength to minister!

The goal of this book is to provide you, the youth worker, with some hands on material concerning a wide variety of problems that today's teenagers face. But these problems are not the run of the mill difficulties that young people face in the normal developmental stages of adolescence. I have found helpful works in areas like: self-esteem difficulties, drug and alcohol use or experimentation, sex questions and concerns, relationship troubles, parental clashes, authority problems, rebellion and so on. These topics are vital to teenagers and a necessary part of any youth worker's knowledge, but many excellent resources on these themes already exist.

No, this book deals with what I call "special-life situations." These are problematic circumstances in the lives, personalities, or bodies of some teenagers. These are the big problems that we often don't see in church youth groups because these kids know that they are not generally welcome. As a result, these teenagers are often overlooked.

A quick glance at the teenagers discussed in this book will reveal the kids who make our hearts ache when we hear about them on the evening news. It is these kids who often come to mind when we see the pain, inequality, and injustice that exist among humans in a sin-filled world. This book is directed to those interested in ministering with these types of youth whether there is just one in your group or ten. It's not an easy challenge.

About the Chapters

Each chapter begins with a true story to describe the type of teenager being examined in her or his own words. In some cases the story is a composite of two or more teenagers' accounts to give a wider, broader understanding of what life is like for those in that particular situation. The story gives each special-life situation a "face," a personality. Names and details have been altered to protect confidentiality.

The story is followed by descriptive and educational materials to provide a reference base. The intent is to give enough professional data to help you identify kids in these special-life situations and to help you understand their world. When available, statistics are given to help underline the drama of some of these types of teenagers.

Also, descriptions and information specific to these kinds of kids is offered. This section elaborates on the "living out" of the description and is intended to be more technical.

Each chapter concludes with suggested programming ideas. These are intended to help you provide all your teenagers with experiences aimed at promoting better understanding.

The Problem of "Perfect" Examples

In this world of special needs, it is not uncommon to encounter shades and tones of variance. In many cases, a clear black and white is not easily discerned.

Not all of the teenagers in your group fall into the perfect "textbook" representation of special-life situations. You may work with young people with two, three or even more special situations in their young lives. The perfect, clinically sound example is more a rarity than a reality.

A child of divorce may have also been abused and be a drug user. You may have a juvenile delinquent who is also ethnically different than the rest of your group. The youth leader must be open and creative. In such cases refer to the other chapters that reference those situations. Perhaps you will find that reading this book and then writing your own combined composite will help you to develop a working "game plan" for the multiple-difficulty young people in your group. We cannot help any teenager if we look at only one situation when it is apparent that she or he is struggling with numerous difficulties.

It is human nature to go after our "pet" special-life situation. Psychologists call this "counter-transference." It occurs when we see in someone else something that is similar to a tough time in our own lives. To correct the hurt in our life, we may try to work it out in the life of another.

For example, when I first began to minister among youth, I was always on the lookout for kids whose parents had divorced. I knew what they were going through. I could relate completely. I overlooked some of the other teenagers and their problems and began to show preference to teenagers of divorce. Finally, a friend asked me for whom I was doing it, the kids or me? Through some self-discovery I became strikingly aware that he had hit the nail right on the head.

It is important to give any hurting teenager some hope that life will get better and brighter. We minister as leaders because we believe in the hope that is in Christ. However, a gardener with three rose thorns in her palm is not truly comfortable until all three thorns have been removed. Rose thorns are removed one at a time, but each demands the attention of the gardener because the pain comes from all three of the thorns.

It is also to the advantage of the youth worker to make a plan of ministry for these multiple cases that integrates the needs of the various problems. This plan will be customized and tailored for the particular situation, based on knowledge as well as compassion.

Noted Christian psychologist, Larry Crabb, says that all humans look for security and significance in life. As believers, we understand that our security is in Jesus and the significance we have is a result of His great love for us. But by providing some feeling of security or significance for a teenager of divorce who is "acting out" as a juvenile delinquent, we will help ease the young person's pain. An initial plan of action might be developed by integrating the descriptions of the two different special-life situations — divorce and delinquency.

The best plan of action is one that begins in small steps and gradually earns the love, respect, and trust of the young person rather than a plan that tries to tackle the whole of that person's life at one time. I have found myself overly worried and concerned to the point that I allowed the entire youth program to rest on my success or failure with one teenager.

I remember that I once encouraged a juvenile delinquent teenager to run as an officer of her class during her junior year of high school. This was one year after she had served time in a juvenile detention center. I imagined that it would be helpful for her self-esteem. She was elected to the office but was a bird not ready to fly. I realized that I wanted this for her more than she needed it for herself. Such outcomes often occur as a result of developing or imposing too large a game plan for any young person.

To implement a plan, begin by:

1) Develop an understanding of the problem or problems confronting a teenager. Read the chapters on the special-life situations that relate to that person's problem(s). Read other reference materials. In this way basic knowledge and understanding is greater than fears, ignorance, and doubts. Information is powerful. Always work to increase your information base.

2) Make this material "real" by personalizing it to the specific teenager with whom you are currently working. Don't turn my story of Josh into your Sara because they are somewhat similar. This is where you add the specifics and details to these descriptions of any given special-life situation. Your Sara is a real person. In helping her, you become a co-researcher on her behalf by making the necessary adjustments and expansions.

3) List small steps in which the goals are to:

    a. establish a relationship with the teenager;

    b. gain his or her trust, love, and respect;

    c. determine the proper avenue by which ministry and integration into your church's youth programs may best occur, (e.g.: Allow a handicapped teenager some challenges in a worship service in order to build her confidence before asking her to share her testimony at the next Youth Sunday);

    d. begin a regular time of prayer support on behalf of each kid;

    e. watch for signs that the teenager is growing or being "squelched." Too much or too little can discourage a young person.

These steps need to be planned, understood, and enacted by the youth leader and the volunteer team with full agreement of the objectives. It is not the kind of thing which you share with the teenager and together you and he or she work on the issues. Charity work is not appreciated by a junior or senior high student with a special-life situation. If we present ourselves as "do gooders" setting out to save the "bad" kids, we will lose the teenagers every time. Jesus brought change through sincere relationships founded in love and respect. Just look at Zacchaeus (Luke 19:2-10) or Mary Magdalene (Luke 7:36-38). This needs to be our model, too.

Finally, all things must be covered in prayer during the time of ministry and long after. Keep a log of your work and pray about your plans, attempts at helping, and so on. Let God minister to you. Ask God for insights and ideas on how each teenager, with or without a special-life situation, may be touched through you with His love. Prayer works. And God commands our presence at His throne. The goal must always be to honor our Lord and give Him the glory. Ask to be His instrument and for the wisdom you will need to minister.

From these steps, the goals can be slowly realized over the course of your ministry with teenagers in special-life situations. Never forget the *Long Run*. God works within us over the entire course of our lives. This is equally true with His work in the lives of the teenagers in our youth groups.

The gift of life is becoming one of my most precious realizations of God's grace. We get a lifetime in which we may work out our walk as believers. We can't become mature believers and powerful workers for Christ in a day. This bit of truth is especially important to those of us in youth work. Our tendency is to want ministry goals that we have set today to be fully and fruitfully realized later this week or...at least before next Sunday's youth meeting!

God gives us a lifespan, time in which we are allowed to work out the details of our lives and walk with God. Should we not allow our special-life situation teenagers the same respectful and faithful consideration?

Implementation steps require time. In many cases that means years. I have worked with special-life situation teenagers and not seen the fruit of change until much later in their lives. They have told me, and deep inside I knew, that the reason they were now doing so well, or better, or great, or even functioning appropriately was because of my interest in their lives when things were difficult. This is not an ego statement of my greatness. Rather, it is a testimony of what God's love can accomplish in the lives of others through ministries yielded to His touch and His direction.

Simply having a youth group in place is not a "given" for success with teenagers who are experiencing special-life situations. There are some tips which need to be in place within the youth program if that program is going to keep and minister to kids with special-life situations. These kids will come and check out the youth group if invited. However, only the group, the program, and the youth leader who are intentionally working to create a climate of acceptance in which all have a chance to participate have any hope of keeping these kids and providing a place where Jesus Christ can change, shape, and guide their lives.

2/ Personal Commitment and Hints for Ministry

I can still feel the want, the need, that I had in those early days of beginning the youth group in Ravenna, Ohio — of hoping that everything would always be perfect.

I had six perfect kids in the youth group who soon began inviting their very nicest friends to join us. The visiting I did on inactive church members with youth group-aged children was going well and those kids were also the kind who would fit right in. Nice kids. It was all so perfect, but it was only a portion of all the available kids in town.

I thank God that this mindset did not last very long and that the Holy Spirit caused me to want, even need, the participation of some kids who were less than "nice" and "perfect." I began to see beyond my blinders to the other kids who needed the gift of salvation and a field where the seeds of faith could grow in fertile soil.

I can't actually remember the first teen who began to make me aware of special-life situations. Truthfully, they began coming so fast that it is somewhat of a blur. I do remember, however, the first juvenile delinquent. He was among the first to plant the seeds in me to want "bad" kids in my youth groups.

Darren was a big kid when I met him. He was handsome, pleasant; one of those kids you liked immediately. After his first couple of visits I got wind of his story. . .and I wasn't at all comfortable with what I heard.

It seemed that Darren had been released recently from a 90 day "visit" to our county Juvenile Detention Center for participating in a number of serious vandalism incidents. One night he and some friends were out drinking and they got a little rowdy. It was autumn and they were walking in the streets of a residential area. They decided it would be funny to rip open the sacks of leaves waiting for pick-up by the city. This escalated and soon the guys decided to expend some energy on the cars parked on the streets. A few windshields were smashed and on they went. Finally, Darren put some rocks through the windows of a house where a friend of his, Johnny, lived. Johnny's family, members of our church, had to replace a large picture window.

These vandalism acts all occurred before I began my ministry at the church. I knew nothing of Darren and was still getting to know Johnny, one of the six charter kids in the group. I was not surprised when Johnny brought Darren to youth group. After all, many of the kids were bringing their friends. And, Darren's sister, Sally, had also begun to attend regularly at the invitation of one of the other charter six.

However, to say that I was stunned to hear the story of Darren's reign of terror and that Johnny's family was one of the victims whose property had been damaged would be to express my shock lightly!

Even now, almost 15 years later, I am still amazed at the love and power of God expressed through Johnny's actions toward Darren.

It wasn't that Johnny immediately forgave Darren and invited him. Actually, the contrary was true. Johnny told me that he held a grudge for quite some time following the vandalism. Johnny and Darren had been close friends before that evening. "But after all," Johnny told me, "doesn't the Bible tell us that Jesus wants us to forgive others?" Well, yeah. . .but Johnny, this guy tried to wreck your house!

Johnny, a junior high believer, follower, and disciple of Jesus Christ, taught me, the youth pastor, how Christians reach out and love those who are so often considered unlovable and worthless. I was amazed. . .and enlightened. . .to the idea that if a new mindset is allowed to operate within the youth, then the youth group may never again exclude anyone intentionally. Four years later, Darren became the vice-president of his senior class and the captain of the football team. Not bad for a "juvie."

A New Commandment I Give Unto You...

The example of Darren, along with numerous special-life situations from other kids who began to attend, brought the items in this chapter to my attention. I began to see some keys to developing a youth program that could be a home and a haven for many kinds of troubled teens. The points are not foolproof or exhaustive, but I have found them to work for many kids who have no reason to visit a church. If they seem a bit familiar, I think it may be due to the similarity these tips have to the ministry of Jesus.

I believe that the church is God's instrument of influence and change on this earth. However, I am sometimes at a bit of a loss to understand why the church remains the focal point of God's plan. We seem to both draw and repel those for whom Christ died. Too often I have seen the church draw those people we perceive to be the most like us — and repel those who just don't seem to fit our particular mold.

I cannot find scriptural justification for selective evangelism! The Bible clearly points out that all humans are sinners (Romans 3:23) and directs us to treat everyone as a potential joint-heir with Christ. First Timothy 2:3-4 says, "This is good, and pleases God our Savior, who wants all men to be saved and to come to a knowledge of the truth." When the problem and the solution include us all, how can we make distinctions and sleep well at night?

I cannot escape from one essential truth in the Parable of the Great Banquet. "A new commandment I give you: Love one another. As I have loved you, so you must love one another" (John 13:34). I find it haunting more than challenging or corrective. The more I grow in Jesus, the more haunted I become. I see how much He loves me, and I tremble because I fail to love others with even a small portion of the love I know in him.

In spite of the delinquency record, the handicap, or the particular troublesome situation in a person's life, we must continue to be loving. And it's not good enough to love out of obligation. It must be genuine. Johnny did, and it brought Darren to Christ. Other kids want the same opportunity.

To give them that opportunity we may need to change our way of thinking. To be effective, we must realize and define some guidelines for ministry which make room in the youth group for those who have no group to call home. . .or for whom their "group" is a gang or other destructive influence.

Guidelines for Ministry

Guidelines are not handy steps. Youth ministry is not that easy or pragmatic. Rather, they are verses of Scripture, attitudes of hope, and contemplations of redemption that serve us well in our work among youth. We have to think and rehearse and preach and proclaim to ourselves first. Then to others. If we don't begin with ourselves, we will soon forget. We can't give away what we don't have.

The following guidelines are not original or that unique. In fact, they may be the kinds of things that you intuitively know. But if they are thoughtfully remembered, they will remind us how not to be, how to be, and to what end in youth work we are to strive.

Be On The Lookout. I marvel at how blind I was in the first few years of my ministry. God would go to all the bother to send me great kids with these special-life situations who would love me and teach me and be patient with me. . .and I would totally overlook the issues of their lives. I would be so excited that another new teenager was in the group that I would miss the special needs of their lives.

I encourage you to Be On The Lookout for those special kids with special needs. God will send them to you, but don't presume that any will come to you and say, "Hey, God sent me your way because I have this special difficulty that you might help me with." Teenagers with special-life situations cry inside to be helped and desperately hope for relief. Yet, they are rarely willing to just let it out. They need help and encouragement. Then they'll share their pain with you.

Even after I discovered what was going on with Darren and Johnny, I did not put together that Darren had self-image problems. And I totally missed that he was a juvenile delinquent. After all, juvenile delinquents didn't attend church! I really missed that one.

Learn about Youth and Youth Culture. Early in my ministry a colleague in youth work told me to, "Read what they read, watch what they watch, know what they know." I think he was a youth ministry genius. Few bits of advice have served me as well.

One of the biggest strengths of youth ministry is to know what is going on within youth culture a good bit of the time. It is hard to hide from someone who knows who you are and the influences you face.

Become acquainted with their culture. It is the only way you will be able to understand:

—The pains, fears and difficulties of those things that are pressuring them. (Remember your first kiss?)

—The temptations they are enduring. (The temptation to drink is always the same.)

—The influences which shape their attitudes, ideas, and notions about life. (Hairstyle is more than hairstyle; it's a statement.)

—The real stressors of their lives. (Peer pressure is peer pressure in any generation.)

Knowing the teenagers in your group is not spying, nor does it mean that you want them to become a carbon copy of you. It only means that you care enough to know those things which influence them during this impressionable time of their development toward adulthood.

For example, borrow or buy a copy of *MAD* magazine to stay on top of the kinds of sarcastic humor that are popular among junior high boys.

Also, skim an issue of *Teen* or *Sixteen* to see what's up with the girls. Some youth workers subscribe to such popular teen magazines. Reading these magazines, as well as others, keeps you in touch with the pressures and issues that preadolescent and adolescent teenagers face.

I also catch MTV fairly regularly to see what styles of hair, clothing, and issues will be coming my way in the next few months. Rap videos and lyrics which call for equality and an end to racism—or else—affect your teens. Music, style, movies, clothing, books, anything that carries the unwritten, "Teenager Seal of Approval" needs to be periodically reviewed.

I often meet with other youth leaders and frequently hear a pastor or director start in with the, "Not *my* youth" or "not *real* Christian teenagers." This assertion is rarely right. It is hard to shelter teenagers from the influences of today's culture...especially those in public school. We teach our kids to be "in the world but not of the world," but it is hard for many of them to resist the lure of what is currently popular. Even if they are not actively participating, they know what's going on.

Being On The Lookout and *Learning About Youth and Youth Culture* are widely sweeping observational guidelines. They tend to lump all of your teenagers together. However, do not ever assume that all of the kids are alike. These tools pick up trends and pulse beats. Each teenager will decide how much, or how little, he or she will actually be influenced. Presenting Christ as the supreme influence is a critical necessity—but our words must be seasoned with grace while we grow in our knowledge of the youth and our faith.

3/ More Tips and Guidelines

The two guidelines in this chapter help us make room in our groups for teenagers with special-life situations. They also encourage the teenagers facing normal adolescent problems and changes to feel comfortable with you and the group.

Be Approachable. This is the old idea of, "I'll be real, if you'll be real." It boils down to questions like: Can your kids really trust you? Can they count on you? Can they come to you if they have a personal problem? Or if they are struggling with a serious special-life situation? A person with a handicap or someone who is being abused will often have obvious physical signs which may tip you off. But what about the sexually abused child, or the teenager whose family is being destroyed by a vicious divorce or alcoholism? Are you approachable enough for them to trust you with this?

Being approachable implies some important personal commitments.

1) Be available. For someone to come and talk with you, you must have time for them. And they have to know you do. Do your kids see you as being

available? Or too busy? Plan some time each week for drop ins. Let your teens know that appointments can be made. . .and that they are *not* an interruption.

2) Be a friend not just another pal, which is about as useful to someone in pain as a casual acquaintance. Larger ministries may suffer here. Let your ministry flow from that relationship. It worked for Jesus! Define for yourself the qualities and characteristics of a friend. Understand how to develop those qualities in your life. And don't leave tough, confrontational love off your list.

3) Be trustworthy. I can't tell you how many times teenagers have come to me with some little "drama" on a Monday, called my wife on Tuesday saying, "I suppose Mark told you all about my run in with the school psychologist for cheating on my math quiz...," and then made an appointment with me for Friday to tell me about the real problem in their life. Why do they make the appointment? Because my wife almost never knows about their little drama. And since I kept their confidence on the meaningless issue, even from her, they knew it was worth a risk on the more serious one. They were testing my trustworthiness.

4) Accept them. Do your teens feel repelled by a fear of judgment or condemnation from you? Who cares if you are "right" about an issue? I find that I serve God and my teenagers best when I listen and accept first, then offer help from our divinely inspired source of guidance, the Bible. To force God's Word on them is not what teenagers need, especially since most of them are still biblically illiterate. They need acceptance, then the offer of direction. Then our lives as a model. Using the Bible as a tool of judgment and condemnation isn't nearly as effective and life-changing as using it redemptively.

Educate the Entire Youth Group. As adults, we have had time and experience to help us work through our prejudices and negative attitudes. Our youth, however, have not had such opportunities yet. Some families may hold a prejudice against a certain group and those attitudes, whether subtle or overt, affect teens on the home front.

Let's say that Janie was raised to avoid anyone who wears blue-tinted sunglasses because they distort the true color of the sun. She is at a disadvantage when any of "those kind" walk into the youth room for a meeting, blue sunglasses and all. This may be her first personal encounter with one of "them."

Janie is going to need some help. She must face the prejudice of her family system, her school pals, her neighbors, and all the others who also judge those with blue sunglasses as inferiors. She will be caught in a crisis of needing to understand why all those others hate the "Blueies" and you, the youth leader, apparently do not. How can you help Janie and educate the group?

The artistry comes in communicating the acceptance of Blueies in a manner that does not denigrate those other relationships in her life while giving her a non-prejudicial point of view. An important factor in your favor as a youth leader is that teenagers are in a natural developmental process of examining and challenging the views of those around them. Parents, teachers, peers, scouts, co-workers, church members...all groups come under their scrutiny as they work to decide what their personal attitudes and views are.

What will the reaction be in your youth group when a Down's Syndrome, gang member, or physically handicapped teenager visits? There is often some natural level of surprise and apprehension among the kids. However, you can moderate the depth of surprise and acceptance by preparing the group in advance.

Heart attitudes quickly become apparent in these situations. Become aware of the potential for problems if your group is so uniform throughout that any variation of color, situation, or physical difference is rejected in thought, attitude, or unkind comments. From the visitor's viewpoint, their own fear of pain and rejection will be foremost in their minds. Think of the impression you and your group will make if that fear is replaced because it is met by Christ-like warmth and genuine acceptance. Such Christian attributes need to be cultivated within the hearts of the kids.

How do you begin reprogramming young hearts and minds inundated by a society that often preaches radically different views? By advertising that "Everyone is welcome here!" But it takes more than simply saying this. It must be continually modeled by the youth leader who provides the group with stretching experiences that bring growth and acceptance.

For example, when our teenagers decided to form a puppet troupe, we took them regularly to the local County Home for the Elderly to perform. Following the programs, we helped the kids interact with the elderly folks. Another time, when I was regularly visiting the Juvenile Detention Center and local County Jail, I would relate some of my experiences to the kids at youth meetings. My weekly visits to minister to inmates became a frequent prayer concern with my youth group.

Of course, the bottom line that must be answered by each youth leader is, "Do we really want teenagers with special-life situations in our group?"

This is a valid and important issue that must be faced. . .to a point. Every youth leader needs to look honestly in her or his own heart for this answer. Yet, I often find that when a problem has a face, the self-limitations and excuses fall to the wayside in the God-given desire of helping the kids with problems.

A teenager came to me once, struggling with the issue of homosexuality. He was the first gay kid I ever met. Instantly, I condemned the young man, silently, in my heart. I knew what the Bible said about homosexuality. However, the trained counselor in me allowed him to share his story. I was touched by this young man's troubled life and decided that I wanted to help in anyway that I could. We talked, we prayed, we counseled, and, finally, I felt comfortable enough with him to invite him to church. Yet, a short time before, my prejudice would not have allowed him to participate with us.

I learned a very important lesson in theology through this. Like the woman taken in adultery whom Jesus did not condemn, I found I had no right to use God's Word to serve my own inclinations. I decided to spend less time condemning a person's sin and failure and place more emphasis on God's redemptive power in Jesus Christ. Both are in Scripture and both are important. But when I allowed the love and acceptance of Jesus to come through, the young man responded to His love and was able to make major changes in his life. He is now married and has a bunch of kids.

Educating the group is accomplished by underscoring the fact that all are welcome in God's family and should be welcomed by God's family.

Specific education comes when it is appropriate. It may not be appropriate to discuss a specific special-life situation when a teenager facing it begins to come to the youth group. Instead, watch the newspaper for situations involving special-life situations and make those articles the focus of discussions and Bible study. The kids are smart enough to generalize the lesson to all people if I refer to one situation as an example of how we discriminate and what God expects.

Group education is essential in every aspect of teenage living. I believe that we often overlook our importance in this regard. The kids expect us to interpret the events of the day in faithful, Christ-centered ways. They are learning how to be believers in a world that is sometimes hostile, always crazy, and often frustrating. Ongoing Christian education programs can make a significant difference.

4/ Knowing — and Accepting

Expect that many of the kids in your youth group have or will become Christians as a result of your efforts. Paul, fully acknowledging that "God gave the increase," also pointed out that he "planted" and Apollos "watered" (I Corinthians 3:6). We, too, need to be honest in our participation in the work of salvation and ministry. I have a responsibility to the gospel. I have been, and still remain, a very important link in the Christian lives of literally hundreds of teenagers. They see me as a Christian example and special point of contact with God. I feel the same way about those who helped disciple me into the faith.

Know the Teenager's Situation. As a significant caregiver to the youth in my life, I must also allow my care to include the problems and special-life situations that develop, or become known to me. Change is a given in the lives of teenagers.

Bobby may have been fine two years ago when he was in junior high, but Bobby is not nearly the same guy now he was then. He has grown physically. He has expanded mentally. He is now in high school which meets in a different building. Bobby is Bobby. But Bobby isn't the Bobby he used to be!

Do you still see him as he was? Or have you updated your perceptions of him over the years? And, under the new, updated perceptions, have you made room in your heart for Bobby's changing life? Is his family still intact? Is he developing a healthy view of the opposite sex? Is he struggling in school? What about the temptations to try substances? If the "real" Bobby were asked to stand up, would you recognize him?

The guideline here is to be continually aware, always updating your information. I remember one teenage girl, Grace, who made a social blunder early in her junior high years. It was a nothing event, but it was funny to others. Of course, the event was always humiliating to Grace. Years later, as she prepared to graduate from high school, I was amazed to find that she had been locked by her peers in a time warp of sorts. They still described her in the context of the blunder. Sadly, I realized that I, too, thought of Grace in terms of the embarrassing event. I realized that I had missed this wonderful young lady's growth because I never let her come into the present with me and the group. She was the Grace I knew in junior high. Not the special person that I now saw before me.

Know their situations, update your mental file of their development, and allow them to become the people that God intends them to be.

Accept the Kids. It is not uncommon to become aware of a particular special-life situation (usually one that is especially difficult for you to accept) and have it be enough reason to form a dislike for a teenager. We are all human.

My friend, Maureen, works with teenagers who are sex offenders. These guys have raped, molested, or attempted to sexually assault others. Many are hard core cases and yet, none are above the age of 18.

She tells me that very few people get involved with these kids. Their situation, because they are sex offenders, repulses most of us to the point of being totally ineffective in any form of ministry or help.

As a youth leader, you need to ask the hard questions of self-assessment. Can you personally accept the retarded? The handicapped? The heavy or skinny? The ugly? The teenaged criminal? The teenager who hates his mom because she left the family for her lover?

Acceptance of others is often a difficult task. This is especially true when the acceptance requires that we remove the rose-colored glasses we so often wear in modern American Christianity. Too often we paint the best representation of the landscape by simply not painting in the telephone poles, litter, rusty cars, billboards, and the like. Those eyesores exist in most scenes. We just don't allow them on the canvas. I think that we, as leaders who are committed to making a difference, need to adjust our attitudes continually. . .especially if those attitudes prevent us from reflecting Christ-like acceptance of a particular teenager.

We are not meant to be infallible as youth leaders, or as Christians for that matter. We are given today by our gracious God to become more like Jesus. To become better people than we were yesterday. What a great gift! And, if we fail, we have the additional gift of forgiveness (I John 1:9).

It is normal and healthy that we occasionally find ourselves at wit's end in regard to a particular teenager or an especially difficult situation.

However, I find that in the tough times, putting the face of the teenager on the problem makes it easier to overcome the prejudice. Ministry without acceptance is about as useful as a plastic wrap windshield on a car. It may repel the rain, but watch out when you turn on the windshield wipers!

As God brings you those teenagers who will stretch you and your ministry, accept them as precious gifts. Some will be major difficulties due to their personalities. Others will challenge you due to their special-life situation. However, work on accepting each. This kind of love must precede any attempt at life-changing ministry. Jesus helped others out of the abundance and purity of His love. Those He touched knew that His motives and intentions were righteous. He wasn't doing it for Himself. He was doing it because He loved and desired that each come to know him as Savior.

The next two guidelines are the biggies. All of the others, though presented first, will rest upon the success of your efforts for these two: Equalize the Group and Reasonable Expectations for All.

Equalize the Group. This guideline is a way of thinking that makes allowance for all. It does not mean that we don't play tag on game night anymore because a teenager is overweight or another teenager has a deformed leg and can't run. Rather, it means that we invent new kinds of tag. A variation of a theme.

Along with regular tag we might play a variation such as "Time Warp Tag " in which a whistle blast indicates when everyone must play tag as though caught in a time warp. At the whistle, all of the players act like they are running through gelatin. Heavy kids and handicapped teenagers now can play with the same ability as teenagers who are athletes.

The game is equalized through a bit of innovation and imagination. Everyone has fun rather than being reminded of some physical limitation.

Equalization is an attitude through which every lesson and activity is examined so that all may participate. I am not so concerned that 32 kids at a meeting all reach the same plateau of experience. Instead, I am concerned that all of the kids have a chance to participate to the extent which they are able and interested. I don't pretend that everything can be fully equal for each teenager at all times. However, I do press myself to equalize the limitations that will eliminate a member.

Equalization ministers to all of the kids. It shows all that the world is not created with any certain kind of person in mind. We may be a predominately "right-handed" world, but the "lefties" are not sitting at the sidelines pouting. They are seeing that things get manufactured for their needs.

Allowing kids with special-life situations a spot in your youth group does not mean that we cater to their particular limitation or problem. No teenager wants to be patronized. We may need to explain some things in greater detail to a slow learner or a teenager with a learning disability. But we don't study or refer only to the simplest Bible stories over and over again to insure their understanding. You might ask another adult to work with the kids with learning problems each week during the lesson to insure that some single concept, rather than the entire lesson, is understood.

Reasonable Expectations for All. Oh, if we could only learn to quit promoting the disease of "High Achieverism!"

It is not wrong to hold expectations of ourselves and others. It becomes a problem when the expectations become "larger than life." Haven't we, as adults, found that we have at times held expectations of our Lord or the Christian faith that were higher than what was promised in Scripture?

For example, in calling on families who were about to lose an elderly family member to the incurable disease of old age, I have often been surprised that some pray for more life. In many cases the person is so old and non-functional, or diseased, that death in Christ is a welcome "graduation." Yet, family members pray and expect God to grant even more life to those who have already been blessed with many good years. It is natural that we die. It is part of God's plan. Still, in the grief of the moment, the expectations placed on God are unrealistic.

Expectations need to be tempered by the "Long Run" concept. In the *Long Run* we will see small, reasonable expectations become part of the lives of our teenagers. Babies begin running by first learning to stand. This is followed by pulling their little bodies around the room by holding on to the furniture and edging with side steps. Later comes those first tentative steps which give way to halted walking. A bit later walking skills are gained and, soon, the persistent child is running. Also included in this package is learning to fall without getting seriously injured.

Falling does not imply failing. As leaders we will sometimes need to give attention to our wounded teenagers. They may be just now learning to stand in their Christian life. The lessons in failure can be tough. Expect them!

Reasonable expectations of a youth program that includes teenagers with special-life situations must be prepared for the times when someone who knows better makes fun of someone who is obviously having some difficulties.

One evening during a junior/senior high mixed dodge ball game, one teenager become angry at the outcome and called another "fatty." The boy receiving the slur was obviously hurt. These guys were friends, and he expected his friend to be a better loser. Yet, a reinforcement came from the incident. I could see the pain in the eyes of the offender at having reduced himself to a level of anger that mocked another. I reminded him that we do not refer to others in such terms, then left the Holy Spirit plenty of room to convict the boy in his heart. The name caller was reminded once again of that "New Commandment" by the Spirit of Christ (John 13:34).

Something needs to be said about modifying our expectations. We do a huge disservice to anyone when we keep them in a little box. We must allow our expectations to change. Expectations that are too demanding are detrimental, but so are expectations that are not demanding enough. No one wants to be remembered for what they could or could not do last year.

My son, Daniel, decided to try out for the high school ninth grade soccer team. As a child, Daniel was a pretty good player in our community's recreational league, but then puberty set in and Daniel began to inherit the height from the German side of our families. This resulted in a time of ungainly "elbows and armpits." He would kick at the ball, miss, and wind up on the ground. He would run for the ball and trip over his feet. Now he wanted to play soccer with the high school team. I was worried for the guy!

As part of the process of being on the team, Daniel had to report daily at 9:00 a.m. for conditioning three weeks prior to the beginning of practice. I thought that this would solve my desire to prevent him from being humiliated. He's not much of a morning person, and he had to walk two miles most mornings to get to the practice field. He went, everyday, never missing. . .even in the rain.

I figured that sore muscles would cause him to drop off the team. He began going to bed earlier during summer vacation to give his body the rest it needed to repair.

I then thought, "Wait until practice begins, with two sessions a day." But he went; he endured.

I finally realized that my expectations for Daniel were far lower than his current abilities when I saw him play in the first game. The boy could play soccer, and he never let up. With tears in my eyes and a chest bursting with pride, I realized that the "little tyke" had pushed his way into "man under construction." He taught me a lesson in appropriate expectations — and updating them when necessary.

Teenagers with special-life situations will need us to have "fluid expectations" for them, too. These are expectations that allow room for lots of change. An abused teenager or a teenager of divorce experiences problems with trust. They need us to keep our word and to resist doing anything that erodes their trust in others any further. Sometimes they may not be able to trust us much at all. At other times they may trust us, experimentally, almost to a fault. We need to expect them to be warm *and* cold. We need to respond with consistency.

The youth group will need to expect that members with special-life situations may occasionally seem unstable in their participation. They may seem unwilling to take part in some of the group functions. It is not unusual for some of these kids to be overly committed one week - ready to do it all with extreme energy and enthusiasm, and unattached, uninterested and standoffish the next. Their lives sometimes become "too huge" and filled with pain. Expect such fluidity. It shows up in the lives of all teenagers. It may be exaggerated in special-life situations. It is over time that healing comes to the wounded.

If teenagers possessing special-life situations are going to become a part of your youth group, it will take time, lots of prayer, and more than a few tears from you. Mistakes will be made. But changes will happen. Miracles will occur. You'll find that the changes will fire your desire to continue. The kids will notice the difference, too. But no one will be more aware of the change in the group than the kids hiding a special-life situation. The changes will provide enough encouragement to prompt them to come to you for some insight or help.

Let's look at some specific life situations as we learn how we can minister to these wonderful kids who sometimes don't fit.

5/ The Juvenile Delinquent Teenager

Megan's Story

Since I'm a girl, no one believes that I could be getting in so much trouble. It's hilarious. I do something wrong and everybody — my mom, the school, the courts — all figure that I don't understand or that I got mixed up with the wrong crowd. They're completely nuts. I get in trouble because that's what I like to do. But let them excuse me. It keeps me out of the juvenile detention center.

I started getting into trouble just after Dad lost his job and started drinking. Nobody wanted to admit that he had a problem. He trusted his company so much. It was beyond him to think that they would let him go after he struggled there for so many years. He sacrificed so much for them, and they dropped him for some young "hot shot" with a degree. Well, Dad couldn't take the humiliation and he didn't know how to be angry about it. He drank until he finally killed himself in a car accident coming home from some bar. I sure miss him.

When he began drinking, we dropped out of church. That was crushing for me because my church was everything. I loved my Sunday School teacher, Mrs. Hazel, and missed her very much. She tried to get our family to return to church, but the embarrassment was too much for my parents. I became angry inside and felt that the rage would boil over and kill me. I began to hate and despise my dad. I wanted to hurt him and Mom for changing my life so much. It wasn't money, Mom still had a good job. It was the huge way in which our lives had changed.

Dad and Mom fought all the time and once I overheard them talking about divorce. I told my brother and sisters and we cried all night. That night I decided to live my own life and to get back at everyone for hurting me so much. Almost the next day I began running with the hoods in my school. We would do small stuff like smoke in school, skip class, and heckle other kids.

As I got older and in high school, the small stuff became crime. One evening I was with some kids who stole a car. After we rode around town all night, they dropped me off at home. On their way to ditch it, they got arrested. Nobody mentioned that I had been with them or I would have gone to court for being an accomplice. Later, however, I got into other kinds of trouble that involved me with the courts. Somehow it didn't matter. It wasn't real anymore, and I had learned how not to feel the pain or shame. I acted the part of a criminal, but inside I was crying.

It all changed for me when Mrs. Hazel died. I had to go to her funeral. It was as if I was being pulled there. Now I see that it was God leading me to go.

I stood at the foot of her casket and cried and cried. She truly loved me and had done so much for me. She understood me and talked to me. I missed her almost as much as I did my daddy. Now, she was also gone from me. I hate to think what would have happened to me if Rev. Cramer hadn't recognized me.

At the casket he came to me and silently stood by me as I cried. After a time he put his hand on my shoulder and allowed me to lean against him. It all hurt so much. Another human to be with was what I needed.

After the service he told me he would like to visit our family sometime soon. I thought it was just more church talk so I told him, "Fine, whenever." Whenever was the very next week.

When he visited, he brought the new youth leader from the church, Tom. Tom talked my language. I was so impressed with his acceptance of me that I promised him I would come to a meeting sometime. I figured it was more church talk. Then, I started getting cards and phone calls inviting me to this thing or that. I was scared that my gang would find out, but I was also scared not to at least try a meeting once. What could it hurt?

I went to a "lock-in" at the church where they were going to have lots of food, music, and some movies. My little brother went with me — he's youth group age, too.

I really dug the evening and had lots of fun. Not the kind of so-called fun I had been having in the gang — stealing, getting high, breaking windows, or giving other kids trouble. This was fun that I would have to call "good." After breakfast the next morning, we had a service that some kids had planned during the evening. I thought it would be so bogus. I can't tell you how touched I was. The hardness in my heart just melted, and I accepted Jesus into my life.

Now I sort of walk in two worlds. The world of my gang and my church youth group. Tom is helping me a lot as I try to figure out what I am doing. It's not as simple as becoming a Christian and just not doing what I've been doing the last couple of years. I'm still a hood, but I also want to be a Christian. More and more, being a Christian is making sense.

The Cross and the Switchblade

In my early years as a Christian teenager I came across an exciting book by Rev. David Wilkerson in which he described his ministry to street gang members. Having had many problems with the law in my junior high days, I remember thinking that God really must be cool to love juvenile delinquents as much as He loves the rest of the "good" kids. In my years as a youth minister, I have found this still to be true.

God loves all of us, even the renegade juvenile delinquent. Yet, as a youth leader, it is often extremely difficult to minister to "Juvies." Initially, they have values and perspectives that can upset the youth program beyond belief. Still, for some of us, the call of God is clearly to involve these kids. . .to confront them with Jesus Christ.

Juvenile Delinquency

Theories of what makes juveniles act out delinquently fill many textbooks and social issues studies. The fact is, some kids simply do.

A behavior is classified as a delinquency rather than a crime based on the offender's age. An 18-year-old is an adult. Below that age, the person falls into the juvenile category. Juvenile delinquency is often not criminal. For teenagers, the problems arise when the behavior is deemed "irresponsible."

Such specific behaviors might include the "devil-may-care" attitude of so many teenagers. As examples, heckling an elderly person on a bus or subway, trying to balance on a car roof and "road surf," yelling at police officers or talking back to school authority figures, cutting classes, curfew violations, being absent from home without consent, using alcohol. Each is an example of behaviors for which juveniles can be held accountable.

Of course, it is not uncommon for these irresponsible behaviors to avalanche toward criminal behavior. A heckling may turn into a gang war or an assault of a teacher. Criminal behaviors may occur among juveniles, such as robbery, murder, rape, and other violent offenses, but provision is made for their age. Sentencing is likely to differ greatly from that of an adult offender. The benefit of the doubt is extended to the teenager as a "delinquent" rather than "teenaged criminal."

Technically, the juvenile offender is not prosecuted by the court system. Instead, the young person is involved in a court decision that may include intervention through a probation officer in the hopes that further difficulties can be avoided.

The causes of juvenile delinquency are not easily understood. It's doubtful that anyone really knows why kids act out delinquently. Yet, there are some clues that help us understand.

It is not uncommon for teenagers to be victims of a feeling known as "relative deprivation." This is the sense of suffering when comparing "my" lifestyle with that of those who have more.

Today's teenagers are very aware of the "haves and have nots." They sometimes react when they feel deprived. Interestingly, this is not just a lower class or middle class problem. Upper class teenagers feel the same when someone has more. For some, the best solution is to act out against the one with more. New cars get spray painted or "keyed" (dragging a key across the paint of the car); windows are broken in homes; property is stolen or vandalized.

Occasionally, we read of a murder occurring because of this sense of deprivation. The violence of the reaction may be a tribute to our society and the influence of TV and movies. The violence is a form of expression by the teenager concerning the inequality he or she feels.

Another factor is the relationship between divorce and delinquency. The best research seems to show that it is too simplistic to relate divorce and an absent parent as the only or best cause of delinquency since many things may contribute. Yet, it is worth watching for while seeking to minister to Juvies. Many juvenile delinquents come from broken homes. Studies show that kids from broken homes are more than twice as likely to be charged with juvenile offenses as would be expected. Be careful not to generalize, but awareness may aid in intervention.

According to Philip Rice in his book, *The Adolescent*, the best factors for predicting and explaining juvenile delinquency are:
- —socio-economic status and class.
- —affluence, hedonism and lifestyle.
- —peer group relationships and influences.
- —neighborhood and community influences.
- —school performance.
- —family background.
- —rapid cultural changes, unrest and disorganization.

This list shows factors and relationships, but it does not allow us to target any one group as most inclined to juvenile delinquency. We can only point to some factors apparent in many juvenile delinquency cases.

Physiologically, some factors occur often enough in teenagers who act out delinquently to warrant notice. Some juvenile delinquents:

• show a delay in development of the frontal lobe of the brain. Fifteen to 20 percent of juvenile delinquents evidence this dysfunction.

• may have organic influences which affect delinquency. Twenty-five percent of delinquents show such organic links as too much insulin, too low a blood sugar count, improper diet, poor vision, hearing, speech and nerve disorders, and difficulties during birth.

These relationships, while not understood, occur in too many cases of juvenile delinquency to overlook their potential for influence. And, it is important to remember that these still do not explain over 75 percent of those teenagers involved in delinquency.

Currently, with the rise of street gangs all over the United States, the relationship between delinquency and gang activity is well known. Gang influence often leaves no choice to teenagers. Either join the gang or face severe physical damage, even death. As a result, many wonderful teenagers become gang members.

Historically, this has been a big city problem. Only a Chicago, New York, or Los Angeles reported such problems. However, now, more small communities are experiencing gang-like activity among the youth. Gangs represent a strong social relationship between peers complete with identity, affiliation, and security — all key issues to today's teenagers. Almost universally, the side effect is juvenile delinquency. And while gangs have traditionally been 90 percent male, the influence of female members is rising in numbers, as are exclusively female gangs.

There is some support to the feeling that juvenile delinquency is rising in direct relation to a declining parental influence with teenagers. As the parental influence declines, the peer influence rises. In the last 10 to 15 years this has been especially true.

Teenagers gravitate toward peers as a reaction to the phenomenon of the "missing parent" in our culture. An increased standard of living has forced many mothers of intact families from the home to work. The necessity for single parent mothers to work so that the family might survive is also a factor. Whether this is the family's choice or not is not our concern here. However, reduced control by parents contributes to a rise in juvenile delinquency. The missing key is the transfer of healthy values from the parent to the children. In many homes, this values influence is peer group dominated.

As an illustration of this, one study quoted by Philip Rice in *The Adolescent*, found that the predominant values among male delinquents were the ability to:

1. keep one's mouth shut to the cops.
2. be hard and tough.
3. find kicks.
4. make a fast buck.
5. outsmart others.
6. make connections with a racket.

Such values are frightening to us as humans, let alone those of us who wish to minister to these kids.

Clearly, helping delinquent teenagers fit into the youth group is extremely difficult.

The Big Question

A new question poses itself to us in youth leadership. It is one that we must face considering the potential ramifications. Simply, are the risks in reaching out to juvenile offenders worth the rewards?

It is convenient to get into an idealistic Christian mentality about this without considering the problems. Each of us must come to terms with the reality that often efforts to reach out to juvenile delinquents fail and, in some ways, may harm the existing youth group. It is possible to say "yes" too quickly with disastrous results.

Among the problems that can arise, it is possible you will see: some kids dropping out, complaints from parents (or at least questions of concern), some concern from the church governing board, resistance from the senior pastor, a negative influence from the delinquent teenagers to the non-delinquent ones. This problem can be so pronounced that you might risk losing your job.

There is no room here for "super spiritual" talk. Jesus did come to save the lost, but He also commands us to "count the cost" of any endeavor (Luke 14:28). If you will lose your influence among those whom you are currently helping — the established youth group — by opening the group to juvenile delinquents, then you need to pray about the door being opened or closed. Let God control this.

Of course, ministry to juvenile delinquents is possible and fruitful and needed. Yet, the "gung-ho" approach will not work with this line of ministry.

A Plan of Ministry

It has been my experience when pursuing a ministry with juvenile delinquents that a multi-stepped format works best. This allowed me to minister to these kids outside the youth group while also including the teenagers already in the group when they were ready.

First, I visited the Juvenile Detention Center for three years and offered a Saturday morning Bible study for those interested. In a short period of time, every kid in the place chose to participate. When the kids were released (some were in for as long as six months), they were invited to come and see me personally, outside the youth group setting. Each teenager had my office phone number (never my home phone) stamped on the cover of the gift Bible we gave them. Since most of the kids were from our area, I thought they would flood my group. Yet, only a few followed up my invitation.

If a juvenile delinquent came to see me, I would usually take them out for a Coke and find out more about them. Some were still "thugs" and I knew that I'd have to spend lots of time with them, one-on-one, before inviting them to youth group. Others were just good kids who made some bad decisions and would fit in easily. These kids were invited to some youth activity that focused on fun. If they functioned well at the activity, I made a special point to invite them to our regular meetings. The "harder" kids were invited to an activity at some point if I felt that their behavior could change.

It would be easy to accuse me of "playing God," but I learned the hard way. Initially, I invited all kids to all meetings all the time. No discrimination or partiality. Small things started getting stolen. Then larger things. Finally, after a lock-in, the youth group had over $600.00 in fund-raising candy stolen, along with the church flags, altar items, paintings, and my entire record collection. I was in big trouble with the church.

Immediately, the delinquent teenagers I had been working with "disappeared." They had been at the lock-in that evening but did not return to any meetings that followed. I couldn't get them back no matter how many calls or visits I made. I knew it was them and they knew I knew. I learned that Christian love and acceptance does not mean that we be presumptuous or stupid.

My faith dictated that I reach out; my heart concurred. That was when I began playing with the "slow introduction" idea of integrating these kids into the youth group. It is an approach which works.

The Bible and Delinquency

Although teenage delinquency does not appear in any specific Bible passage, law-breaking is found throughout. Since we are all sinners, it is equally apparent that we have all fallen short of God's mark. Yet, instead of running with the sin theme, I find it more beneficial when working with any teenager to discuss the encouragement in Christ and the wonder of His love that reaches through our failures.

Many delinquents actively and often willfully commit some act that may be categorized biblically as "sin." Yet, we must remember the verses concerning sin which reach out to redemption. In Psalm 25:8 we are told, "Good and upright is the Lord; therefore he instructs sinners in his ways." Psalm 51:13 is equally encouraging in ministry to the juvenile delinquent: "Then I will teach transgressors your ways, and sinners will turn back to you." This is good news because we are assured that we who have gone astray are redeemable. Sometimes we forget.

In Matthew 9:10-13 we find the account of Jesus eating with "sinners." He was greatly criticized by the religious leaders of His day for doing so. His glorious response was, "I have not come to call the righteous, but sinners." Luke 5:32 adds to this declaration that He came to call "sinners to repentance." There can be a turning around for delinquent teenagers. It is found in Jesus Christ!

It seems plain that Christ did not differentiate between the lawful and the lawless. He looked into the heart and saw kingdom potential in all. Yet, sometimes we discriminate against juvenile delinquents because they already have points against them. Jesus accepts them, but He also reminds us to be as "shrewd as snakes" (Matthew 10:16), to recognize proper fruit (Matthew 7:16-20), and not to cast "pearls to pigs" (Matthew 7:6). There is nothing wrong or unspiritual about being cautious.

I believe in ministry to juvenile delinquents. It can be fruitful and life-changing. I have seen hardened teenaged criminals come to Christ with hearts full of repentance and walk away from that encounter changed people. I have marveled at God's power as I watched teenagers with court records as thick as a novel ushering and taking the offering during a church service. Kids destined for jail, lives of crime, or social dropouts let the healing power of Christ's love make them new creations and, in turn, went on to be the class president or youth group leaders. God changes lives.

Programming Ideas
For the Youth Worker:
1. Read such works as *The Cross and the*

Switchblade by David Wilkerson or *Run Baby, Run* by Nicky Cruz. Ask at your local Christian bookstore for other titles that represent stories of changed lives. Look for books on God's ability to change the lives of delinquent youth. These books will inspire, inform, and confirm your burden to reach out to these hurting teenagers.

2. Visit the Juvenile Detention Center in your area. Talk to professionals who work with delinquent teenagers daily. Find out what motivates them, what gives them hope, what frustrates them. Try to get in touch with their reasons for helping these troubled youth. It helps put things into perspective. If these folks see delinquents as worthy of the investment of their time, we, seeing their souls' needs, may find the same.

I have had eye-opening conversations with juvenile lawyers, judges, case workers, probation officers, jailers and others related to the juvenile justice system. Too often these folks are seen as just "doing a job." In actuality they are often inspiring people who have a concern for youth and believe that changes can be made. As Christians, we may sometimes disagree upon the means of changing lives since we find our basis for change in Jesus. Yet, we can support them in their work and cover them with prayer.

3. Inquire if some kind of visitation or Bible study can be set up in a Detention Center in your area or any network residence youth home it may operate. Many Centers have satellite "Group Homes" for teenagers who come under the custody of the court system but who do not have delinquency records. Generally, they are considered "unruly" and not in need of incarceration. Offenses usually range from runaway (often to avoid incest or abuse) to

extended truancy. These kids are under court protection.

Holding a short term series of Bible studies or discussions focusing upon spiritual matters is a good way to assess if this area of ministry is really for you. A summer study or some series in conjunction with Easter or Christmas is a good, closed-end format. Knowing that the program will only be offered for a few weeks gives you an "out" if you should need it. Remember, there is nothing unspiritual in finding that ministry to juvenile delinquents is not for you. Don't be a martyr. Be sensitive to the Holy Spirit's leading. God may be preparing someone else for that position.

4. If you are considering a ministry to delinquent teenagers and have investigated the possibilities as suggested above, then one of the most basic things to do before beginning such a ministry is to hold a "heart-to-heart" talk with your senior pastor, the official church board, youth group parents, and other concerned church members. Don't spring it on them after the fact.

Instead, enter this area of ministry with full disclosure and communication. Take the "small steps" approach described earlier. It will aid your endeavor if you share the ministry with them. Challenge them to pray, to volunteer at the detention center, to begin a Christmas gifts program or to start a library at the center. Ministry partners are more useful than ministry antagonists. Begin a ministry to the families of the offenders.

5. Spend some time in the library and research the dynamics of juvenile delinquency. We have only skimmed the surface. Read about such suspected contributions to delinquency as conduct disorder, abuse, chemical dependency, abandonment by one or

more parents and related themes. This time in research will be invaluable in your understanding of the delinquent teenager.

6. Try to enlist ministry partners to accompany you when you work with delinquent teenagers. My best friend, John, helped me in my visits to the Detention Center for over two years. We could share the teaching, the visitation and, later, debrief each other. His support helped me to keep going. Plus, more kids were able to be influenced since there were two of us to spread out among the kids. Jesus sent His disciples out two-by-two. Team ministry has its advantages.

For the Juvenile Delinquent:
1. Aside from beginning a program or Bible study in a detention center, you could also set up a "mentoring" program through the church for interested delinquents. It is amazing how well some of these kids respond to love and attention. It is life-changing in many cases. Assigning a responsible, mature man or woman to a hurting teenager can work wonders. Be careful to make sure that the assignments are male-to-male and female-to-female.

Some training will be essential for volunteers. Focus upon communication skills, the nature of delinquency, and appropriate gestures of love. There is a strong danger that the "mentored" teenager will fall in love with the mentor as this, in many cases, is the first love ever shown.

The responsibilities of a mentor are numerous. Foremost, mentors are to be friends to the delinquent teenagers. To listen, to take out for a Coke, to call or drop a note from time to time...simply be a friend. Additionally, mentors may offer to help with school work or sit with the teenager in church. Sometimes a ride may be needed to a youth meeting.

Also important for mentors will be the "interpretation" of the Christian faith, the rules of the youth group, and other transitional things which may be new to a juvenile delinquent who is just beginning to grow in his or her faith. These kids often become frustrated simply due to the embarrassment of a new and unknown situation.

2. Offer a special and separate small group for the delinquent teenagers you meet. A weekly or bi-weekly meeting for these kids will help them express their frustrations, hurts and concerns. As with any small group ministry, they will begin to gain a sense that they are not "going it" alone. Some of these kids are so tightly bound inside that being allowed to speak out is a new experience.

3. Remember things like birthdays, graduation, or other special days in their lives. Even a card is special when you are locked up or when you have no supportive system. These simple gestures make an incredible difference.

4. Plan activities which mix the rest of the youth group with the delinquent kids. Too many isolated "delinquents only" events will cause them to be suspicious of your intentions. Are you there for them or to keep them away from the rest of the kids? Again, this is precarious work as you find the balance between integration of the two groups.

Mixing and eventual integration of delinquent teenagers into the regular youth group is important because of the peer transfer of values. While many delinquents "know" good values, for example, that stealing is wrong, they lack a reason not to steal. Seeing their peers practice healthy values works to establish values within themselves.

Simple social activities in which all the kids discover something new together work well in integration. It takes off the edge of competition which some delinquent teenagers may feel toward the other kids, and vice versa. Visit a new show at an art gallery. Or take a museum trip together. Plan a weekend work camp or a lock-in at another church. The point is to make the experience a new one for all of the kids.

5. One of my "secret treatments" is to invite delinquent teenagers to church camp. I get concerned folks to help pay for them and send them off to a week in which they can be the person they really want to be. It has worked phenomenally in reorienting their lives. In many cases, the week at camp is the turn around. Many never act out in a delinquent fashion again. (Keep in mind, some rebellion and acting out is typical for the adolescent years and not necessarily delinquent.) This is not to say that the kids became "perfect." Rather, they no longer seek to be criminal.

For the Entire Group:
1. As juvenile delinquents become integrated into the youth group, it becomes important to focus upon Christian values. Some regular, "good" teenagers find juvenile delinquents very exciting. There is the chance that they may "stray." Also, the rescuer mentality may develop in some as they set out to "save" the "lost" delinquent.

Spending time encouraging and training all the kids in what we value as Christians is time well spent. Don't simply focus on "right and wrong" issues. Look at justice, racism, peace, forgiveness, and grace. These are topics in which all believers need a strong foundation.

To maintain a successful group any and all "speciality" groups must be made to feel as though they are part of the entire group, not a splinter group. The delinquent teenager must feel as though she or he is as valuable a part of the group as the most average member. If this is not conveyed, the small group participants (whether juvenile delinquents, children of divorce, low income kids or any other group having a particular problem) will feel patronized and either revolt or drop out.

2. If many of the teenagers in the youth group come from problematic home situations, try an annual discussion or unit upon the fruit of the Spirit (Galatians 5:22, 23) and the fruit of the flesh (Galatians 5:19-21) within the context of the larger discussion in Galatians 5 on our freedom in Christ. Freedom is not a license to do all things and anything. Many "church kids" somehow miss that message.

For example, teenagers often miss the concept that freedom has limitations. God gifts us with a free will, but that is not permission to act out as we want. Training teenagers in Christ-like self-discipline is a great investment in their spiritual futures.

3. Be certain to advance some trust to delinquent teenagers as you would any other member of the group. That is not to say that the best job for a teenager with a record of robbery is the treasurer for the group. However, it might be appropriate to allow this teenager to carry the money and pay the check out clerk as you do the shopping for a youth group cookout. You make a strong statement of trust to her or him that is not lost upon the rest of the group.

4. There can be the tendency to watch delinquent teenagers once they are integrated into the group.

This is not entirely a bad idea, but don't let the delinquent teenagers know it.

One year I invited a girl to church camp. We had to pick her up from the detention center in order to take her. While she loved the church camp experience, she was unable to immediately break her habits of behavior. Throughout the whole week (one of the longest weeks of my life!) she tried to seduce various guys. My staff and I had to watch to make sure that this young lady and her "target of the moment" stayed out of the woods without her knowing that we were watching her. God be praised, we were able to thwart her every time, but it wasn't easy.

At risk were her feelings, her self-esteem, her reputation at the camp, and her possible commitment to Christ. She simply did not know how to behave otherwise. It was our feeling that she should not be punished for not knowing, but we couldn't allow her to act out, either. We had a responsibility to teach her biblical values. Such is the balance of ministry to juvenile delinquents.

5. Conduct some Bible studies in the regular course of the year focusing on some of the Bible characters who were renegades and lawbreakers but who also experienced the touch of God. People like David (with Bathsheba), Moses before he left Egypt, and the Apostle Paul make wonderful studies. Be sure to note for the kids the blatant honesty of God's Word and how the Bible hides none of the "seamy" sides of God's "servants under construction." I don't recommend glorifying the delinquent behavior in these Bible characters. Simply point out God's redemptive love which encourages sinners to repent. The stories of Absalom and the sons of Eli make good

character references about the consequences of unchanged behavior in delinquent kids, too.

6. Have the whole group establish a Code of Conduct. Decide what is important to the group and what behaviors need to be observed by all members. Issues such as smoking, drinking and other teenager temptations are likely to come up for discussion. Lead the kids in a biblical consideration of standards and let them form their conclusions from that study. If you feel strongly about an issue, feel free to interject, but let them own the Code or they will not abide by it.

Some issues will be church policy. Those must be included. It may be helpful to have the senior pastor explain these.

After being developed, the Code of Conduct will serve as a guideline which gives you some strength when you have to intervene in a problem. It is better to establish a rule before the first occurrence than later when someone will have hurt feelings.

This chapter investigates the joys and challenges of reaching out to juvenile delinquent teenagers with the gospel of Jesus Christ. It is a message of hope and liberation that delinquent teenagers often want to embrace. However, the catch is that these kids need a flesh and blood representative to communicate this Good News.

The special-life situation of juvenile delinquency is a complex and dramatic one. The kids can be hard and abrasive. It is not an easy focus for ministry. However, it can be one of the most rewarding aspects of youth work. There will be heartbreak, confusion, and fear. But, more often, there will be the inexpressible joy of seeing a life changed. God is faithful if we try not to be fearful and full of excuses!

6/ The Substance Abuser

Tony's Story

Life in my family was never ideal. We lived together in an emptiness. Not distant or intimate, angry or friendly — just empty.

My family isn't close. My parents travel much of the time with their careers. Since I'm the "baby" of the family I have nothing in common with my sister and brothers. Our age differences are too spread out. We have nothing in common. Life is a big zero.

To pass the time I would often pretend I was an adult. I did adult things like stay up late, watch what I wanted on TV, and visited the liquor cabinet.

At first I didn't drink enough to even get a "buzz." I wasn't looking for a high and the stuff tasted awful. . .I was just playing around and sipping. But as I approached my teenage years, the lonely boredom of life became my greatest nightmare. I started to drink more to dull the hurt inside. It worked.

Soon I was drinking almost daily. Then I began to hide some of my parents' alcohol in a "stash" of my own. Eventually I was caught drinking at school — a drink I badly needed.

When confronted by school officials and my parents I was able to convince them that I was just playing around. They believed me and treated it like no big deal. I got a warning at school and a two week grounding. But nothing changed. Life was still boring and lonely.

I continued to drink without getting caught. I tried some drugs and, while they were somewhat interesting, I preferred alcohol's "buzz."

As time passed, my grades dropped. Too many late nights, too much memory loss, too much personal apathy. My parents put me in a couple of detoxification programs and lectured me. Even my sister and brothers talked to me about how embarrassing it all was to the family. What a joke. Suddenly, I'm the family problem and everyone wants to help. But no one wanted to help me on the inside where it hurt.

In my junior year something happened that was both wonderful and a problem. A friend became a Christian and, before I could resist, she got me to attend a youth meeting. I didn't want to go, but I didn't want to disappoint her either.

Surprisingly, I liked the meeting very much. The adults were caring and seemed genuinely interested in me. It was really cool!

In the weeks that followed I, too, became a Christian. It has proven to be the best decision I ever made. I have a new faith and hope for my life, new friends, and some strong support. But here is one fear. I wonder what Doug, the youth leader, would say if he knew I still drank sometimes. That's the big problem that has accompanied the blessing.

I try to quit and I promise God daily that I've had my last drink. But I slip so often. The drink is something I need.

God has been good to me. Why can't He take "the taste" for alcohol away? Why can't I wake up one morning and no longer be an alcoholic? I feel so bad. I'm such a failure as a Christian. I wish I knew what to do. If only there were someone to talk to.

Tony is just one of millions of junior and senior high kids in the United States who are battling a dependency on drugs and/or alcohol. He comes from a good family, with reasonable values, yet he feels unloved and neglected. He is becoming more devoted to his newly found faith, yet he finds that his dependency is not magically disappearing. He is a good kid with an all too common problem. Is there a place for Tony in our youth groups?

Tony's dependency on alcohol developed from his need to numb the emptiness he feels as a result of his family's busy life. The euphoric high and dulling stupor that alcohol provides anesthetizes the ache in his heart.

Reasons for Chemical Dependency

There are an estimated 3.3 million kids between 12 and 17 who have a serious drinking problem. Millions more are considered moderate or experimental users. Contributors to substance dependency read like a psychology text. Many are a direct attempt to cover something that bothers, hurts, or confounds the abusing teenager.

• Lack of love and loving feelings within the home. The oblivion gained through substance usage covers the truth that the teenager feels unloved.

• Feelings of emptiness concerning family relationships, purpose, and life goals. Alcohol and drugs are used to fill the void.

• Poor standards within the family concerning drinking and drugs. When the parents have their own usage problems, it dramatically increases the chances of abuse among their children. Over 50% of all alcoholics grew up with at least one alcoholic parent.

• Cover up from a traumatic event that negatively affects self-esteem. Many teenagers begin drug and alcohol usage following an event such as rape, molestation, divorce, a death, or the like.

• Peer pressure. Being accepted by one's friends always plays a dominant role in the motivation to experiment. Teenagers still do what their friends do.

• Media attitudes. Some studies link the suggestion of TV and movies as a factor in teenager substance abuse. Drugs and alcohol are often seen as exciting. Too many "heroes" slug down a six-pack before saving the world.

• Availability. On many school campuses the teen can buy drugs as easily as purchasing a school lunch.

Other reasons include curiosity, teenage dares, attempts to hurt parents, or to make a statement of independence. Usage may be aimed at boosting self-esteem or for the "fun of it." Through it all, we see a needy teenager reaching out for love.

Scripture shows a church in which human suffering is eased and God's children are comforted (II Corinthians 3—7). Yet, we must never make the erroneous assumption that the act of salvation or being raised in a church exempts anyone from the frightful dangers of substance abuse. The heart of Jesus compels us to reach out to those teenagers suffering under chemical addiction.

In my work with substance abusers I have found that teenagers need encouragement and support as they work toward recovery. That is why such programs as Alcoholics Anonymous (AA) and Narcotics Anonymous (NA) have so many success stories. Both programs encourage the user in a loving and caring manner to believe in him or herself and to work at overcoming the addiction with each new day.

Be assured, the world's greatest youth groups have alcohol and drug experimenters and users in them. Church kids aren't exempt from life's temptations. Some of your teenagers have either experimented or are using substances. For the Christian teenager, the pain is doubled as they feel the guilt of willful sin and wrestle with letting God and the church down.

The numbers concerning teenage use of alcohol and drugs are frightening. In reading these statistics, keep in mind that there is almost no difference in the numbers when studying churched and non-churched kids. Alcohol and drug abuse are the number one young adult problems today.

Statistics on Substance Abuse and Teenagers
*When 25 percent of our nation's fourth graders report feeling pressure to try drugs or alcohol, it is easy to believe that 90 percent of high school seniors and 50 percent of seventh graders have actually tried these substances.

*Thirty-one percent of our high school students are considered to have a serious misuse problem indicated by drunkenness at least six times a year with 66 percent admitting regular use.

*Almost 10 percent of high school students are daily users of drugs or alcohol with 15 percent drinking weekly with five or more drinks per occasion.

*Average age of beginning to drink is 13.

*Drunk driving is the leading killer of teenagers ages 15 to 24.

*There is very little difference between the drug and drinking habits of males and females in the teen years.

*14 teenagers die each day in drunk driving accidents with a total of over 10,000 teenagers a year. Another 130,000 are injured annually in drunk driving accidents or about 15 kids per hour.

*Alcohol is by far the leading drug of choice for our teenagers yet 57 percent admit to trying at least one illicit drug before high school graduation.

*Half of all teenagers who drink heavily use marijuana at least once a week. Six percent have tried cocaine.

With teenagers themselves reporting that drug and alcohol abuse is the biggest problem facing them today, we would be naive to assume that our youth are not among these numbers. Better to assume our kids are at risk and work to educate them than to assume they are somehow immune to these temptations.

General Suggestions

Knowing that substance abuse is a real issue for your teenagers is the first step in reaching them. The following are useful clues to identify substance use and abuse among your youth.

• Physical indications such as bloodshot eyes, slurred or incoherent speech, irregular muscle control like not being able to walk straight or poor balance.

• Alcohol on the breath is still a good tip off.

• Absenteeism from youth group activities among active teenagers.

- Missed appointments, a sudden hostile attitude toward you or the group, and failure to follow up on their responsibilities.
- Discipline problems such as lying, arguing, and failure to keep their word.
- Is there a sudden interest in non-churched friends, often older, or running with a new crowd?

Obvious changes in social actions, physical appearances, and personality worth noting are:

- Sudden bad grades or poor school attendance.
- Hyperactivity, drowsiness, or forgetfulness.
- New or increased depression and uncharacteristic mood swings.
- Changes in appearance, money problems, reports or confessions of hallucinations or delusions, attempts to borrow money, and cravings for junk food.
- Other clues include: tremors, drug paraphernalia (cocaine spoons, cigarette papers, or marijuana holders which are worn as jewelry), increased isolation and secrecy, decreased family involvement, caring less about school, work, church, friends, sports, hobbies.

Of course, some of these changes are common in the teenage years. But the more symptoms that a teenager displays, the more likely that he or she is struggling with chemical dependency. Take the signs seriously.

It is important to distinguish between teenagers who are experimenting and those who are regular users. Experimentation may mean some irregular use and then the teenager quits. Addiction means the young person is unable to control the problems and will likely need intervention and professional help.

Shaming or condemning abusing teenagers is likely to estrange them from the youth group. They already live in so much guilt and confusion, they will decide that they don't need any additional headaches and leave the group.

Our goal is to make a place where these kids can fit in and find the commitment to Christ more fulfilling than the temporary buzz. They need the love and support of our youth groups. Hope is what can make the difference between a life ruined and a life redeemed. Jesus Christ, working through us, is hope.

Programming Ideas

For You:

1. Attend an AA or NA meeting. The experience is often illuminating and uplifting. Meetings can be found by looking up Alcoholics Anonymous in your local phone book and calling for an open meeting. This is a meeting that anyone may attend. Meetings are non-threatening and completely anonymous.

2. Attend an Alanon or Alateen meeting with the same agenda as above. Here you can get information about what the rest of the family feels. You'll gain insight on various family patterns that drug or alcoholic families construct to hide or ignore their problems. And, your level of ministry competence will rise significantly.

Both of these groups can provide you with helpful information and materials. While reading it, keep in mind that they are presenting their specific positions and they are not biblically centered. Sometimes there is criticism that these materials are not scientific. They are still great resources.

3. Develop a file on various types of drugs, their effects and characteristics, the specific dangers, signs

of usage, and so on. Update this file regularly. The drug of choice can change as rapidly as styles of clothing.

Materials can be obtained from state or local police departments, local alcoholism programs or boards. Keep a file of newspaper clippings to tip you off about trends, changes, research, and other aspects of the current chemical abuse scene.

Visit the closest treatment center to your area. Currently, the trend is to specialize, so the local center may be for teenagers, adults, women or men only. Some centers work with any abusers.

Learn about detoxification and rehabilitation. Some centers will allow you to sit in on various open sessions. Usually they offer good community education programs throughout the year that will be valuable. Information is a valuable tool in the battle against chemical dependency.

5. Know thyself! What is your personal opinion and practice concerning alcohol and drugs? Are you leading a double life? Do you have your own problems? Time spent in personal reflection and prayer will reap dividends in your ability to minister to your teenagers.

To Help the Using Teenager:
1. Before you can help a using teenager you must first become her or his friend. You must be trustworthy and the teenager needs to feel comfortable with you before you try to help. Knowing about drug and alcohol abuse won't make you a good counselor. You must also know something about people and hurting hearts. Therefore, show an abusing teenager the acceptance of Jesus.

Being a friend is especially important with substance abuse because the substances can alter the teenager's perceptions. Jackie, a regular at every meeting, may not be able to think clearly through the haze of alcohol. While you may be willing to help, the using teenager needs to be willing to be helped.

When approaching a teenager you suspect is wrestling with chemical dependency or experimentation, never take an accusing posture. It will only build a wall of resistance. Spend some time with the teenager and find out what's going on in her or his life. Be open and available and often the opportunity will arise to put forth some hard questions.

Begin with, "Brad, I've noticed that your attendance at youth group had been infrequent lately. You seem tired, a little irritable, and withdrawn lately. Because I love you and think so much of you, I don't want to ignore the possibility that you're having some trouble. If you want to talk, I'll listen."

Brad may or may not respond, but drop it there for now. You've made contact as a true, supporting friend. Stay in touch and show lots of love. When the trouble comes to the surface — and if it is drugs or alcohol it most definitely will — you are in place to reach out.

2. When the usage problem becomes known you can be a major part of the solution. Working with the family, offer to accompany the teenager to AA or NA meetings. Be as much a part of the recovery effort as you can be. If rehabilitation is necessary, visit the teenager regularly. Most importantly, keep the teenager in the youth group. He or she will need the love and support that the body of Christ has to offer.

To Help the Youth Group:

1. Work to take the edge off temptation by sponsoring various after-event parties at the church for your teenagers and their friends. We used to open our church gym following home football games to give the kids in our community a place to hang out. It proved to be a valuable buffer for the kids who came. They had a place to go and a reason to miss the parties where drugs and alcohol were likely to be offered.

2. Bring in speakers as part of your annual youth group curriculum. This is a spiritual issue for teenagers. It is more than a drink or a joint. It is one of the major ways teenagers succumb to temptation, and it is a manifestation of all that is un-Christian to our youth.

Professionals can educate our teenagers about the real-life drama of alcohol and drugs. Most speakers have examples galore. However, avoid guilt manipulators who try to "make" the kids resist for all of the wrong reasons. Most teenagers will make good choices if they have good information.

I have found excellent speakers through the state police, the local police, alcohol treatment centers, and through the school system. Seek professionals who can speak as Christians. When this is the case, the program is even more effective. A police officer who is also a Christian and openly talks about it with the kids makes a double impact. They receive a program on drugs and alcohol while also learning that God's people work in many areas of life.

3. Discuss the complexity of the substance abuse problem with your teenagers. Help them to see how many are hurt by addiction in the family. Jobs are lost; money is wasted; the family reputation is hurt; faith is damaged. Teenagers often need to be

stretched beyond cut and dried beliefs. Help them develop compassion and a vision to see the wider effects of any problem. Substance abuse is always a family problem. . .including the family of Christ.

4. Give the problem a face. Kids are far more likely to understand if they can attach a real-live human face with whatever problem you are studying. Who in your church has undergone treatment for a substance abuse problem and come out on top? If they are comfortable and willing to share, you'll have one of the best programs imaginable.

Hearing someone tell their story will reach the users and non-users in your group. The users will learn of the risks of alcohol or drug use and some ways out and the non-users will find more meaning in saying, "no!" Both groups of kids get the message that this youth group seeks to be a caring family for all teenagers. Hearing another believer share their story of addiction, treatment, and recovery from within the church speaks powerfully of the power of Jesus Christ in changing lives...and the consequences of unchecked sin.

5. Sponsor an overnight retreat centered on alcohol and drug education. Open it to the schools in your area. Often the chemical rehabilitation center closest to your area will send speakers or lead the whole program. Parents are usually willing to pitch in with food, meal preparation, chaperoning, registration, and the like. This problem is of great concern to them, too.

The great thing about programs offered to the community through the church is that they hold massive evangelism possibilities. While we did not openly "preach", we did make it clear that we, as a church, were concerned about our community and the children. We let the parents know about our other Christian education programs. Families are drawn to churches that don't hide from the tough problems of life. Be ready for lots of visitors!

Finally, this type of program is a wonderful prevention tool. The kids learn skills in turning down offers to use drugs or alcohol. They learn about the harmful effects and the rigors of recovery. They meet some real people who have lost so much and fought to regain their lives. If carefully planned, these overnighters are wonderful successes.

6. Lead the kids in an exhaustive Bible study of such words as wine, drunkenness, and sober. This is important because so many kids seem to know that Paul told Timothy to drink wine (I Timothy 5:23). They love to throw that one in your face!

Educating ourselves and our youth group members concerning substance abuse will be a great help in winning the war against drugs and alcohol. The problem will arise among your teenagers. Remaining calm and responding with love and concern from a base of accurate information is powerful. Reactionary comebacks based in fear only alienate abusing teenagers further. Jesus was not shocked by the world around Him. He did not recoil from problems. He firmly stood His ground and spoke for God. Amazingly, He did not condemn any except Pharisees. He called all to a changed life and led the way for them to follow. Introducing our teenagers to such a Christ is a marvelous joy! Today's teenagers are waiting to meet Him.

7/ The Abused Teenager

Lisa's Story

Dad left to find work in Michigan. . .and never returned. It's been 13 years since I last saw him.

I was all Mom had. He left when I was four. Mom made me the center of her hurting world. I see now that she used me to get through her pain of my dad leaving. She used to talk to me, take me places, and be real attentive. That's why I was so confused when the hitting began.

I was about eight. Mom was still a single parent and needed to get a job. She was always tired. She'd come home, say she needed a nap, and sometimes sleep through to morning. We had food so I could find something to eat. But the loneliness was killing me. I was starving for love and attention.

The first time she beat me was when I wouldn't let her "nap" before dinner. I played outside her bedroom door, making noise to get her up. She yelled a few times but I ignored her. I wanted to see her. I was alone all the time...from getting home from school until I fell asleep. She was dead tired, but I needed my mom.

She came flying out of her room and began to smack me, over and over. I screamed for her to stop.

She did and clutched me to her, crying and begging me to forgive her. It was the first time she had held me in years. I held her, enjoying the attention — but not the pain. That night, though, I learned how to get Mom to spend time with me.

Over time the beatings continued. The time together did not. Now it was just the hurting. Mom acted like a caged animal when she was home. I learned to be quiet and careful. I was afraid of the beatings. I resented her and felt guilty when she began to date. I was relieved when she was away.

Last year the bad got worse. Mom began to date a guy who stayed at our house a lot. When Mom had to work overtime, he would come over to "check on me." I don't know exactly how it happened, I think maybe I've blocked some of it out. Anyway, the guy started touching me under my shirt and tried to do things to me. It was terrible. I couldn't tell Mom; she would never believe me. I had no one to talk to or tell. Soon after, he did more than just try touching me.

When Mom decided to marry this guy, I suggested that I go live with Grandma. I knew Mom would love this idea. To her, I was just in the way and Grandma was family. I thank God Grandma agreed to take me. Later, I found out that Grandma suspected that something was going on but had no idea what to do. She's the one who started bringing me to church.

I don't see Mom much, and I won't see her husband. I'm trying to figure out how I'm going to live with the memories of the abuse. I don't need to relieve her guilt. But I heard her telling Grandma that she's ready to have me back. No way! I'd take that issue to court. I have a new life now, thanks to God, my grandma, and the church.

I have bad dreams sometimes. I get real mad and want to scream. Sometimes I feel like God let me down by allowing this all to happen. But I'm learning that God didn't do the abusing and that He will lead me into healing. That's why I like church and youth group. There's a family here for me. My only fear is that someone may find out. Then I'm not sure if I'll be allowed to come anymore. Maybe the rest of the church won't want me. Until that comes up, I've decided to enjoy my new life!

Lisa is not the only teenager who has been emotionally, physically, or sexually abused in my youth group. Little does she know that others have had similar battles. Even teenagers from good, Christian homes may find themselves battered. For now, Lisa has found the home she always wanted in her church family. Yet I wonder, as she does, what would happen if others found out about her abuse?

The world of abuse is dark and secret. It is a world often overlooked and ignored. Our inability to help is overshadowed by our lack of knowledge as to what we should do. Yet, the children call out to us for help. And there is much we can do.

The Facts and Figures

Teenage abuse occurs in four major areas: the psychological, the physical (which includes neglect), the sexual, and through the destruction of personal property. While some areas are more evident than others, the truth is that teenagers feel so badly about any abuse they will go to great lengths to cover for the abusers. In their fear and pain, they perpetuate their own difficulties. Often their friends participate in the conspiracy of silence. Thus, the concerned adult who can help often doesn't find out about the abuse for months or years.

The history of child abuse is fairly recent. It was not until pediatric radiologists began noticing irregularities in the X-rays of children in emergency rooms that the area received any attention at all. The X-rays revealed unreported, older injuries in children who had "accidents." In some cases, broken bones that had not been set and severe tissue damage could be seen. Some of the radiologists became curious and began comparing notes. Their reports brought the secret world of child abuse into light. Other findings show:

•The most frequent reasons given for abusing kids are discipline, religious beliefs, and to force education.

•The majority of abusers are the natural parents. In abuse, 55% of the cases involve the fathers, while neglect is caused by mothers 68% of the time.

•When surveyed about being abusive to their children, 68% of the mothers and 58% of the fathers questioned admitted being violent at least once in the past year.

•Studies of juvenile delinquents and teenaged offenders showed that up to 87% had been abused as children or teenagers.

•Delinquents are abused five times more than non-delinquents.

•More than 1 million kids are abused or neglected annually in the United States.

•Over 3.2 million American children and teenagers live with their grandparents and other caregivers to avoid abuse or neglect from their parents.

Reasons for Abuse

There are no good reasons for abuse. Having said that, let's be even more honest. . .it is not easy to maintain balanced mental health each and every day. Our families struggle with bills, schedules, burned suppers, church meetings, report cards, arguments, missed dental appointments and all the rest. We become frustrated and angry. The media seem to communicate that problems are solved by violence. Cartoons and action programs present violence as the fastest and most direct means of conflict resolution. We learn to hurt in order to gain control.

For this reason we must respond with love and kindness, not contempt or horror, when encountering an abusive situation. Discovering that the "Smith" family, active in church, is having family violence problems should not throw us off balance. Rather, we need to commit ourselves to ministering healing and work with the family. Take note, however, that abuse problems are best handled by trained professionals. Our role is one of support and encouragement. We can also be very helpful in making referrals.

As families weather such "storms of life" (Matthew 7:24-27), they can take great comfort in the support their church can offer. Families can grow through this difficulty.

Sadly, abused teenagers often see themselves as the reason for abuse. It may be inconceivable to many kids that their parents are dealing inappropriately with their problems. This is especially true of junior high teenagers. It is not uncommon to encounter a teenager arguing in favor of their parents.

When asked, "Why do you think your parents abuse you?" younger teenagers may state such responses as: not picking up after themselves, not making their beds or cleaning their rooms, not accepting responsibility, or forgetting a chore. One fellow told me that he sometimes gets, "a look on my face" and so, "Dad hurts me." His solution, "I don't look that way around Dad."

Older teenagers employ a more sophisticated denial to the abuse. It is common to hear such "reasons" for abuse as: being out too late, forgetting to call home, doing poorly on report cards, or not cleaning the car after using it. To the abused teen, not playing well at a sporting event, acting silly or immature, and even smelly socks can be enough to justify the abuse. The attempt is to keep the abuser in some kind of "good" standing. Kids need the love of their parents. They will do almost anything to preserve and maintain that love, even when it's a facade.

It is interesting that many of the "problems" teenagers cite may require parental discipline. We might say that "Mr. Jones" is right in his efforts to mold the behavior of his teenager. The problem comes in the manner, nature, and severity of the discipline Mr. Jones uses. Parents have a right to discipline their children both legally and scripturally (Proverbs 13:24, 19:18). God disciplines His children (Hebrews 12:3-17). But He is never vicious or unloving.

A line between discipline and abuse exists and can be crossed by parents. When anger enters discipline, there is the danger of injury. Being human, we all become angry. Our Christ-like response is the barrier between love and abuse. But any family, Christian or otherwise, from the pastor to the most infrequent member, is at risk for potential abuse. Discipline should mold, not damage, our children.

Parents have similarly imaginative reasons for abuse — all of which are equally bad. I have heard of moms being ticked off by what the boss said and beating the kids. Or, "the kids were arguing," or, "their rooms were messy." Loud music, bad grades, being caught smoking, forgetting chores, all of these and more are given in defense of abuse. Even worse, they are sometimes presented in the guise of Christian discipline.

These may be valid reasons for Christ-like discipline, but the response is totally invalid and unacceptable when abuse is used to solve the problem.

A bruised and battered child has not been disciplined. They are victims of criminal assault.

General Suggestions

There is no standard type of abuser for whom you should be on the watch. Yet, some factors do seem to indicate that teenagers in certain settings, living under certain conditions, have a higher likelihood of being abused. Being aware of these associations will help you to increase your awareness of potential abuse among your teenagers.

Surprisingly, young people are abused by mothers almost as much as fathers. This is because mothers spend much more time with their kids. Add to this the fact that almost 50% of America's children live in single parent homes, most often with Mom, and this becomes more understandable. It is not that women are more abusive by nature. Men tend much more toward aggression in their problem-solving. But moms and kids are together more.

Other factors that may increase the possibility of abuse are:
- —younger parents
- —single parents
- —unwanted pregnancy
- —difficult childbirth
- —other young children at home
- —low education level of parents
- —parent with health problems
- —child having health problems
- —parent not having any personal free time
- —socially isolated family
- —irritable or unresponsive child
- —poverty
- —unemployed parent
- —general, unresolved stress

The presence of these factors do not "make" a parent abusive. But some adults never learned the coping skills to handle such stressors.

Looking for signs of abuse among your teenagers is no easy task, either. They can become very adept in covering the evidence of abuse. However, some signs of possible abuse are:
- —often seem to be scared
- —act somewhat paranoid
- —clothing is inappropriate for the weather, such as long sleeves in the summer which may be hiding bruises
- —more aware or concerned with their surroundings
- —strange attendance patterns, such as coming to a youth group event very early and staying as late as possible, or a regular attender who misses meetings for no apparent reason
- —seem to prepare for pain, such as flinching when a hand is raised or if someone moves suddenly

—extremes or swings in behavior, such as crying often, acting fearless or fearful of adult authority, dramatic "glad to sad" ranges in attitude

—need for physical touch, as if starved for it

—disruptive, hyperactive, demand continual attention

—sudden changes in character and conduct

—regression into more immature behaviors

—seem to take on an adult or parent role

—often remark how great their family is, or, inversely, often express hope for a new or better family

—poor physical condition, such as being dirty or unkempt, skin sores, signs of malnutrition, pale skin with no natural luster, lacking normal strength, poor dental care

—learning disabilities or lapses and delays in normal development

—physical signs of abuse such as bruises, cuts, burns or welts, and broken bones which are said to have come from "accidents"

Keep in mind that these signs do not automatically mean that the teenager is being abused. If a number of factors do show up in any particular teenager, though, it is wise to be concerned and attentive. Don't "let it slide" and assume all is well.

What Should Be Done?

Plan an abuse intervention strategy before it is needed. Talk to your pastor and church board and form a policy which plainly states how the church will treat suspected or confirmed abuse among teenagers and children. Make this very public.

If you suspect a teenager is being, or has been, abused, don't sit on it. In most states you are legally liable and could be prosecuted if it is discovered that you had reasonable knowledge and ignored it. For this reason you need to talk to a lawyer or social service agency about the particular laws in your state concerning church workers and the reporting of abuse. Having a plan and knowing your legal commitments will serve you well in ministering to your youth.

There is no perfect intervention plan should you discover that a teenager is being abused. Your responsibility will be to report it. Then the proper authorities will take over. Face it, you might make a bad call. You could lose a key church family. The teenager might lie or exaggerate. These things can, and do, happen. But the alternative is far more severe, legally and to the child, should it be discovered that you did not report abuse. This is to say nothing of our responsibility before the Lord.

If a teenager comes forward, the whole issue is more direct. Here are some considerations to guide you.

•Reassure and listen. The teenager coming to you is scared and will need desperately to talk.

•Believe the teenager. Don't seek to verify accuracy. In almost all cases teens who come forward are telling the truth.

•Find out the facts in a calm manner. Don't panic, act disgusted, or confused as to what you should do.

•It is important that you not convey the idea that the teenager is at fault or act like she or he somehow deserved the abuse.

•Let the teenager know that other kids also get abused by loved ones. It helps to know that others face the same difficulties. Reassure them that there is nothing about them that caused the abuse.

• Never promise confidentiality. Don't agree to be part of the ever-present "conspiracy of silence" that teenagers often hold.

• Feelings need to be discussed and allowed.

• Privacy must be respected when they feel your questions for clarification are too probing. Leave the details to the authorities.

• Remain supportive, present, and accepting throughout the entire event.

• Be aware of what the whole event is doing to you. Abuse issues cause us to feel revulsion and anger.

Our Savior died for all, not just those with more "acceptable" sins. Pray for the teenager, the family, the authorities, and all that will happen following your report. And pray for yourself that God will give you strength, discernment, and all of the qualities you will need to bring resolution. Thank God that your personal involvement may have literally saved a young life.

There are risks in reporting abuse. You may be threatened. Some will say it was none of your business. I am aware of some youth workers who have lost their jobs. Yet, your legal, moral, and spiritual responsibilities remain unchanged.

It is likely that someone in your youth group faces physical, emotional, psychological, or sexual abuse. Taking a stand instead of ignoring the abuse will make your youth group a special place of safety and caring for all of the teenagers.

Programming Ideas
To Educate Yourself:

1. Do some reading on the subject. It is easy to locate free information through social service agencies and library books. Check under such

headings as family violence, abuse, sexual abuse, and domestic violence.

2. In many areas seminars and workshops are offered by university, law enforcement, social service agencies, hospitals, and church groups to provide abuse information to the community. They are often free or very affordable. Make use of such educational opportunities.

3. If a Christian university, college, or seminary is nearby, check to see if the psychology, sociology, or criminal justice departments have any resident experts on abuse. Some schools may offer classes on family/domestic violence or abuse.

4. Spend some time in self-reflection to discover what you feel about abuse. Were you abused as a child? Did you come from a very supportive or nurturing family? How might these different experiences color your understanding of abuse? We must know ourselves, as leaders, before we can be of much help to others.

This became very important to me during a joint retreat between my youth group and another. The other youth leader, I knew, had been abused as a teenager by his parents. During our retreat, he lost his temper and began treating the kids in abusive ways. Without thinking, he was treating others as he had been treated. Soon after, he lost his job for physically and sexually abusing teenagers in his group.

To Help the Abused Teenager:
1. In general, let the kids know you are aware that some of them may be abused and, if ever desired, you (and your spouse) will be available to talk about it. Whether the abuse is past or current, your gift will be to let the teenagers know without

asking that they did not deserve the abuse. Lead them into healing by reinforcing a healthy understanding of who they are in Christ.

This subject is very taboo in our culture. The kids will not usually bring it up unless they feel the door is somehow open to discuss it. Talking about it, even acknowledging that it happens, does much to remove the taboo and begin ministry. When I first allowed for the reality of abuse, I had four cases suddenly appear over the course of that summer. Prior to that, no teenager had ever come to talk to me about her or his abuse.

2. Before actually needing the services of an abuse support group for teenagers, investigate to see if such a resource is available in your area. Try to find a Christian group. Unfortunately, most of these groups are for adults. If one meets regularly, take some time and get to know the leaders. Then, when and if a teenager comes forward for help, you will have a powerful tool of help to offer.

If no such group meets in your area, pray about starting one through your church. Enlist the help of a local Christian counselor or psychologist and see what can be developed.

3. If abused teenagers are active in your group, it will be essential that your group be "user friendly." Your group can become a place of peace and safety by discouraging aggressive and hurtful behaviors. Make the group aware of situations that are threatening to some. Help each member to imagine what life would be like if the norm was the fear of being hurt.

This is not to eliminate great, rowdy games or active sports. Rather, it is to put youth ministry in a proper perspective. If some wish to play an acceptable game that may threaten a teenager of abuse, offer an alternative activity. Not only will the abused appreciate your consideration, the uncoordinated and sports-haters will love you, too! A "kinder, gentler" youth group will be appreciated by all.

4. We developed a "Kindness Club" at one point to change the hurtful dynamics of our youth group. Teenagers can lash out with great skill and mastery. Hurting kids were being further hurt by their Christian friends. Any act of aggression, abuse, or ridicule was greeted by a loud cry of "kindness!"

Encouraging the group to remind each other about one of the fruit of the Spirit will do much to maintain the good feeling that the youth group is safe. This can become a special gift to the abused teenager.

To Help the Whole Youth Group:
Many kids will be clueless about abuse. Occasionally offer exercises to help the whole group understand. Here's one.

1. Divide your group into teams of three to five members each. Advisors are welcome to participate. In each group, assign family roles which represent the varied families of today such as a mom, dad and 2.5 children, single parent family with mom having custody, the same with dad having custody, a family with one parent traveling much of the time, a family with a grandparent living in the home, and so on.

Before the meeting, write some of the real problems today's families face on slips of paper. Consider such tensions as racism, poverty, a parent in an unfulfilling job, unemployment, alcoholism, chronic illness, delinquency, and truancy. Have each group pick one, and in some cases, two, of the tension slips.

Direct the groups to dramatize what such stresses may do to a family. How would a parent feel day-after-day? What about the kids? Encourage them to focus on feelings.

Ask each group to assume various family positions or prepare assignments and have them pick their roles. Allow them time to interact in role-playing their character, the stress, and possible reactions. Suggest that one of the outcomes be abusive, but don't allow such theatrics as fake hitting. Have the group describe what it might be like to be hit viciously by someone whose love you crave.

Challenge them to investigate non-abusive resolutions. Act out that scenario. Discuss why the abuse may have occurred and what worked differently in the resolution role-play. Leaders should feel free to "turn up the heat" if the portrayal turns into a clean cut sitcom outcome. Help them to be reality-based about the tribulations of daily living, yet challenged by the promise of Christ's presence.

This exercise is good in raising the understanding of abused and non-abused kids alike. Both see that abuse is a complex issue and can appreciate the inadequacies of abuse as a source of resolution. The message is clear: abuse is never a solution.

2. Study abuse in the Bible with the group. God's Word condemns abusive behaviors. But you may have to dig a bit to get the message.

Look up "abuse" or other words such as "violation," "hurt," "pain," "perversion," "offense," and "misuse." Let the kids research the verses to decide what the Bible says about abuse. Then, discuss a Christian's response to abuse. Close by noting that it is a complex problem with no easy, quick answers. Be available for further discussion.

3. Bring in a Christian professional in the field of abuse. An evening featuring a number of experts who work in various abuse related fields makes an even more compelling meeting. A program coordinating the services of a lawyer, a minister, a judge, a police officer, a social worker, victims of abuse, and a room full of kids has amazing possibilities. Each speaker would share their relationship to abuse and their professional responsibilities and perspectives.

The message to your youth group is that this is not a taboo topic. They become educated and equipped. You are sending a message of acceptance to the abused teenagers and to those who may lean toward abuse as a form of problem-solving.

If nothing else, you will enable your teens to help their peers seek help, not hide abusive situations. They will know that it is not "loyalty" to keep those kinds of confidences.

4. If you have a working relationship with someone from the group who has been abused, is in recovery, and can talk about it, you'll have a life-changing program. Older, former members of the youth group often hold places of honor with the younger members. Their testimonies can be a significant influence.

"Rachel" or "Scott" returning to the group to discuss their personal, living torment makes it hauntingly obvious that Christian teenagers can be victims of abuse. Younger teenagers, feeling that it is something they did, discover that they aren't "bad" after all. Chances are, they'll seek help.

5. Assign various agencies which distribute information on abuse to groups of teenagers for investigation. Have them contact the groups on behalf of the larger youth group for whatever free

information they have available. Two months from making the assignment, set up a reporting night and distribute the materials to each teenager. Let the whole group read through their materials together and allow time for open sharing of statistics, reports, and what the materials say. Sometimes the statistical numbers will not be in agreement. Discuss why. Affirm that mismatched numbers and disagreeing studies do not dilute the problem.

6. Explore various kinds of discipline that are not physical. It is not your purpose to undermine parental authority or to change the way a parent disciplines their children, but you may influence a potential abuser to seek some alternatives for discipline and punishment when they have kids of their own. Abused kids tend to abuse their own kids.

7. Plan a Bible study on discipline. Compare what the Bible says about discipline, training, instruction, and rules. The Bible contains fabulous insights on true, biblical discipline, correction and punishment. Seek the counsel of God's Word and make it clear to your young people, too.

Abused teenagers have lived lives that few of us can imagine. The physical and emotional pain that they have experienced and continue to endure, as well as the constant fear and rejection, make our hearts cry out to God to bring them relief. Don't assume that you are not the answer that God is sending to that prayer. Rather, assume that you are and reach out with the hands of Christ in caring.

8/ The Homosexual Teenager

Rob's Story

I don't think I set out to be gay. I can't remember a time in my life when something happened to turn me against girls. It just sort of happened.

During high school I was sort of backwards. I wasn't interested in dating, but I loved hanging out with my friends. Especially at youth group. We did so much together as a group that dating never occurred to me. Most of my friends dated, and I had some girls that I especially liked. But I never felt a need to ask anyone out. There was always plenty to do with the group.

In my junior year I attended a school function with my English class at a university. It was a study program which included many high schools from our area. In the dorm the first night I was talking to a bunch of guys late into the night. Someone had brought some beer and I was stupid and drank some to be cool. Later in the evening some of the guys started touching each other and then someone began touching me. The experience turned into my first sexual encounter, and it was with another male.

Now I find myself living a double life. I've been with other guys and a few people are learning of my homosexuality. I have so much to lose but I can't seem to stop. I still love God and go to church but I'm not sure that I should. While I feel dirty inside, I'm also not sure I can stop. Nothing in my life has been so confusing.

Cheryl's Story

I was first sexually touched as a girl by my troop leader on a camp-out I attended as part of an all girls organization. I never told anyone but the experience changed me inside.

Later, in high school, I began having a sexual relationship with my softball coach. To my surprise, some of the other girls on the team were also lesbians or had leanings toward that lifestyle.

Lesbian. It's such a scary, harsh word. I heard it again last week during the sermon when the pastor declared that "Lesbians and gays reject God's love and commands. And God rejects their sin." Did I ever sit up in my pew. How can this be? I never miss church or youth group. I have been a Christian almost my whole life. I don't know what to think anymore.

I'm glad I can still come and talk to you. I know that you don't approve of my lifestyle, but I feel your acceptance of me as a fellow believer. I'm not sure where all of this will lead, it's not like it's a "I hate men" thing. And I always pictured myself as married with a bunch of kids. What's going to happen to me?

The Controversy Rages

In a recent seminary class I listened as fellow students debated the issue of homosexuals and the church. We were a very mixed bag of conservatives and liberals. Just about everyone, from Baptists to Methodists, fundamentalists to Episcopalians, mainline denominations to independents, was part of the group and debate.

As I listened to the debate rage on, I was aware that as a group, these struggling future church leaders were not sure what should be done with homosexuals in the church. Some felt comfortable in declaring that they automatically go to hell, period. Others felt that the scientific world was beginning to find evidence that it was biological and, therefore, part of God's creation. Someone mentioned that Jesus never spoke to the issue so didn't that prove that He was not concerned about it? Another countered with Paul's condemnation of homosexuality in Romans. One sister compared the condemning verses to the hundreds of verses which call us to look to the needs of those wrestling with sin. So many views, so few conclusions. Yet, I praised God that people of faith were talking about this issue.

In my ministry I have had the opportunity to work with a number of homosexual teenagers who were not comfortable with their sexual choice. Some practice a gay lifestyle in opposition to what they genuinely feel or believe.

In the New Testament, Paul wrote Romans 1:24 — 2:4. Here, God calls homosexuality a shameful lust, an unnatural act. Then He follows it immediately with a stern warning against judgment and a reminder of God's kindness and patience. It is the context of chapter 2 which puts Paul's comments into perspective and urges us to reach out.

We must be careful that while we love the person, we do not tell them it is all right to continue in that lifestyle. God's Word must be our final authority. This chapter will not help you with those who openly display their homosexuality. My experience has taught me the difficult, painful lesson that the militant homosexual will not hear and does not want to hear what God's Word says.

Our burden is to look at how to help those who have entered a lifestyle that is not what they were seeking. These may be the confused, the abused, the seduced. These young lives hold out the greatest hope for change.

The Attitude Of The Other

Jesus says, "In everything, do to others what you would have them do to you..." (Matthew 7:12). In these precious words we discover what psychologists call empathy, or putting my feet in the shoes of someone else to figure out what his or her life feels like. Empathy is very similar to what we, as Christians, call compassion. Love is what brought Jesus to die on a cross. Compassion characterized every aspect of His earthly ministry.

When some of my favorite youth group kids came forward, fully trusting me, and admitted their lifestyle, I knew it was time to look into what they were going through.

And here is where the gift of compassion comes in. Through compassion, sorrowing for the sufferings of others with the desire to help them, I attempt to come to grips with what life would be like for the hurting person. Working with homosexual teenagers in my youth group, in private conversations, I was able to gain many insights on what was going on within them. I felt that to reject them would be an additional confirmation that the church today is no longer relevant or able to help.

Like any sin, God expects the sinner to confess it, to turn away from it, and to accept Christ's cleansing. His blood shed at Calvary covers all sin.

On Being Homosexual

The causes of homosexuality are very unclear in spite of the "facts" that we so often read in the popular press. For males, this development is thought to occur in adolescence. In females it materializes a bit later, often in the college years. Again, doing your own research is probably best. However, I imagine your conclusion will be: "who knows?"

Numbers and causes aside, to minister to these kids you must be willing and able to step outside personal feelings and prejudice. This does not mean that you no longer hold your convictions. Instead, they do not hinder your compassion to the hurting homosexual.

In dealing with the homosexual teenager we are again confronted with an area that is outside of the expertise of most of us. Refer these kids to a trained, Christian professional but do not allow that professional to replace you. Remain a key support in their lives. Working through this problem takes time.

More Considerations for Ministry

We cannot look for clues to recognize homosexuality. There are none. Homosexuality is found in just about every type of person, race, and culture. No body characteristics, hobbies, diet, vocation, socio-economic qualities, or background reveal homosexuality. Every imaginable group of people can, and often does, have homosexuals in it.

If we are to minister to gay and lesbian teenagers, we must first start within ourselves and decide if,

God willing and helping, we will be able to help these kids. Revulsion, homophobia, or the inability to look beyond the behavior to the individual is the root of violence and hatred against them.

I believe that this is what "forces" some homosexual teenagers to the lifestyle. Persecution often makes martyrs out of regular people. If you react to a questioning kid with disgust, anger, or rejection, you may further entrench her or him in the lifestyle. Keep in mind that these kids are teenagers first. That means they will rebel against an adult authority that tries to make them do anything. Our ministry, as pointed out in Philippians 2, is to adopt the mind of Jesus in all matters.

And what would Jesus do? Each of us, based upon our relationship to and understanding of the Savior, will find our own answers to this question. But use Scripture as the foundation of your decision. The whole counsel of God is essential for a solid, biblical base.

What would Jesus do?

— Jesus would not reject them.

— Jesus would talk and listen to them.

— Jesus would love them.

— Jesus would be there for them.

— Jesus would care for them.

— Jesus would point them to God.

— Jesus would say, "Go, and sin no more.
　　Neither do I condemn you."

When I am asked by a homosexual teenager for help, I make a conscious effort to separate the issue of sexuality from the teenager. Separate, not dismiss. In doing this, I find that I maintain my perspective. I found that I simply had to quit looking at the gay or lesbian in terms of their sexuality. I had to see the person.

Surprisingly, you may be clueless to the homosexual leaning of a teen who trusts you enough to tell you about this problem. If so, don't feel as though you've failed with your spiritual radar. Homosexuals don't necessarily take on the masculine female or effeminate male persona.

Try to find out why they decided to come and talk to you. Have they been caught by parents or peers? Are they afraid? Is there an AIDS infection possibility? Do they feel they have betrayed God? Are they seeking information? The reason is essential to a good, helping relationship. Work from the point of their need.

Admit to the teenager that you are not a trained therapist but that you would recommend that they see one, a Christian one. It is a good idea to have this reference on hand in advance. Offer to accompany the teenager to any appointments.

Sometimes teenagers enter a gay or lesbian relationship because they do not feel that they fulfill self-imposed standards of what it means to be male or female. Because they miss that goal in their minds, they think they are inadequate. Rather than be rejected by the opposite sex, many report it is easier to relate to the same sex. This is homosexuality that can be changed because it is an unconvinced self-image of the teenager.

I recommend two things here. Professional, Christian counseling, if they will go. And treating these kids as if they were your own child. How would you act, as a believer in Jesus Christ, if this were your son or daughter?

I do believe that we can reach out to these kids and make room for them in our youth groups. Some of us may have active homosexual youth in our groups now. But since they are used to hiding so much of the time anyway, they often attend unrecognized.

When we work with a teenager who is involved in a homosexual relationship that they report enjoying, or when we have teenagers who want to be homosexual, we face different issues. Frankly, these teenagers make tough cases for change. They certainly are not outside of the realm of possibility for God. Yet, they don't see their homosexuality as a problem. This is when we must look carefully at the issue of church discipline and the impact on the youth group and the ministry of the church.

As a closing story I want to tell you of a young man who came to me for help. "Glenn" was a vibrant, handsome young man in his first year of college. How he became gay is not important. However, after some time he decided he was not sure of his gay-ness. He began to wonder about it. This became even more complicated when he became a Christian and got involved in a college Christian fellowship.

Through a friend, Glenn came to talk to me. He wanted to be different. He wanted me to tell him that it was OK to change. So many had told him he would be denying his true self to quit his gay lifestyle. He was looking for support and acceptance, not more fuel for a fire he no longer wanted to feed.

Glenn wanted to change and had the strength to do so. He needed a supporting push.

No area of ministry is likely to be more frustrating. Yet, our homosexual teenagers need us. Be there with the love of Christ for them.

For You:

1. Learn as much as you can about homosexuality — and AIDS. Your local library is a wonderful source for developing some helps for your homosexual teenagers.

2. Study what the Bible says about homosexuality and determine what you believe. The Bible is our final authority always, but it may help if you can picture some of your dearest teenagers as gay or lesbian. This gives the problem a face.

This is not to say that we change Scripture. We simply need to make sure that we continue to offer the redemption it promises. We cannot afford to establish our own "unpardonable" sin.

3. Realize that few topics in Christianity are as volatile as this. For many of us, the special-life situation of homosexuality is a problem-filled issue. There is probably no more sensitive topic within the church.

I suspect that many will read this chapter first. Why? Because the nation is wrestling with this issue. Our teens are being bombarded with it as an acceptable, "alternative" lifestyle. It is hard stuff. While recent studies estimate that only 1-2% of the population are homosexual, your teens are confronted with the media's endorsement of it daily. If we are to stem this tide, we must approach the subject with openness, seeking a fuller understanding. Ask God for illumination and sensitivity.

4. Enter this area of ministry with full disclosure and communication. Take the "small steps" approach described in chapter five for working with juvenile delinquents. Begin a ministry to the families if possible.

5. Try to enlist ministry partners to work with you when talking with these teens. A husband/wife approach will keep you from any false charges as well as present God's perfect plan for love between two humans. Jesus' two-by-two approach to discipleship is good advice here. Team ministry has its advantages, especially if the teen comes from a problematic home situation. Plan a time when you and your wife can disciple the teen as a couple.

I believe in ministry to homosexual teens. It can be fruitful and life-changing. I have seen confused teenagers come to Christ with hearts full of repentance and walk away from that encounter changed people. I have marveled at God's power. Christ's love makes new creations of us all. God changes lives.

For the Homosexual Teenager:

1. Along with your pastor and youth advisors, make the youth group a haven of Jesus' love — but be prepared to tell them about Jesus' tough love. God does not wink at or tolerate a willfully disobedient lifestyle from any who claim His name.

Then, keep their sexual struggles very confidential. Most youth groups will become divided if a gay or lesbian teenager emerges from the ranks. Don't think it will be wonderful if you can get "Stacy" to come out of the closet and express her "true self." This happens in some youth groups today. It is destructive and exploits the teenager. Helping these kids should be a confidential matter.

2. Many kids "become" gay or lesbian after a same-sex experience early in adolescence. At a sleep-over or a camp-out, they have some level of sexual contact, usually petting, and they either get labeled

or label themselves as homosexual. This simply is not the case.

One or two sexual experiences with the same-sex does not make one homosexual. Discovering if this was the case for your gay or lesbian teenagers can be immediately successful in re-directing their sexuality. I've seen this occur many times. Scripture tells us that we are as we think of ourselves in our hearts. If we can change that manner of thinking, we can often change the person.

3. Work to find out if the homosexual behavior masks another problem. I have worked with kids who used homosexuality as an outlet in dealing with anger, abusive parents, major school difficulties, problems in the home, neglect, and other issues. The homosexual behavior becomes a vent for problems that seem unsolvable.

This is understandable. Many adults engage in extra-marital affairs for similar reasons. It is common to find that the affair is only a symptom to another root, such as anger or a feeling of sexual inadequacy.

The same may occur among some of our teenagers and their personal issues. However, don't think that a couple of weeks of family counseling will fix everything. Realize that the teenager may have developed a new self-image. It may be years before he or she decides to seek change.

4. Work to instill within the gay or lesbian teenager that Jesus Christ forgives unconditionally (I John 1:9) and wants to offer or to restore fellowship with Him. To know that forgiveness is offered as often as we ask is a wonderful gift of grace for all of us. We cannot think that it somehow excludes homosexuals.

My heart breaks when a new kid, struggling with this special-life situation makes his or her way to my group with a nightmare story of rejection at the hands of God's people. I've worshiped with teenagers who have raped, murdered, robbed, beaten, and sold drugs. Or been victims of such. They were heartily accepted. But Jesus Christ had changed them. They had turned from that way of life.

Why limit this offer of love? Change will come only by the power of God through the love of Christ if it is going to come at all. It will not come through my insistence and demands. Struggling people often fail to hit the mark. We can all attest to that. Graciously apply that reality to gay and lesbian teenagers. Lead them to Jesus. Then lead them into a life of obedience to His will.

For the Whole Youth Group:
1. Begin to expand the awareness of homosexuality (which is sodomy) among the kids. Don't reduce biblical standards or raise a banner that the homosexual lifestyle is problem free. It is not.

2. Discuss the issue of AIDS with reference to the homosexual. Just last week a gay, HIV positive man who runs a program for HIV persons in our area told me that today 75% of AIDS patients are gay men. However, in 10 years most of them will be dead. In that same 10-year span the disease will move into the teenage and women groups. It is now. These two groups are the fastest growing risk groups currently.

While AIDS is still a homosexual issue, it is also a good springboard for working in the risk among teenagers who still, for the most part, assume that they will not have to worry about AIDS. It happens to other people. Sadly, it is becoming a heterosexual problem, too.

3. Offer an open discussion on homosexuals and the church. Does your church have a position? How about the senior pastor? Perhaps your senior pastor would make a good moderator of the discussion, pointing to the current world view of homosexuals, the Scriptures, and the balance between judgment and grace.

4. If this would be effective with your group, consider visiting a hospice of people dying from AIDS. Put on a skit, sing songs, have a Bible study. This may open up many eyes that have little compassion for those with the disease, provide an opportunity of ministry, and change some young minds.

Too many young people today have bought the "politically correct" viewpoint of extreme acceptability, a "preference," an acceptable expression of sexuality. While most do not want to embrace it for themselves, they believe that the gay or lesbian person has a right to choose their form of sexual expression.

As leaders, we are very uncomfortable with that news. If this attitude will change, it must begin with us. Rather than recoil and ignore, talk about it. Don't slam the door on opinions. Keep in mind that teenagers are trying to figure out these kinds of issues. Often you hear what they last heard on TV. Give them a chance to work it through with the larger group. Give them biblical foundations that will not only moor them, but also allow them to help their peers.

5. Contact a local Christian counselor and ask him or her to come and share from his or her counseling experience. What has this professional discovered? What stories has he heard? Let her

guide the group in working through the anxiety and confusion of this important topic.

Gay and lesbian teenagers are afraid. They feel and fear rejection. They have few places to call home. The goal of ministry to these teens is to reorient their lives. This does not mean they become perfect overnight. Rather, they no longer seek to define themselves as gay or lesbian.

The turnaround from such a lifestyle may only begin if you let them have a place in your youth group. There the love of Jesus Christ may reach and draw them into seeing their "lifestyle" for what it is and God's holy love for what it is.

Being there for these kids is as much a part of the Great Commission as any other group that needs our ministry.

9/ The Learning Disabled Teenager

Bryan's Story

I saw my school file once by accident. It was sitting on my teacher's desk and my name was on it so I picked it up and read it. I guess this was in junior high, so it's been a few years. Anyway, next to my name it was marked "LD," and I didn't know what that was. Inside, a sheet stapled to a test said I was learning disabled. So that's the big LD. I'm so dumb I can't even learn right.

School has been tough for me all my life. I hate to sit still as long as they expect. I can't keep my attention on any topic as long as they want me to. When I am asked a question or given directions, they don't sink in. Tests are a nightmare — I don't understand what's being asked. When the results come back, I hide my tests and look later.

The guidance counselor says I'm bright, even above average in some subjects, but I'm always just a few points away from failing. I understand what's going on in class, but I have trouble getting the answers out. I feel so much pressure from the frustration that I get upset and want to explode.

Sometimes I take it out on my friends and end up in the principal's office. Mom and Dad certainly know my principal.

When asked what I want to be, I always get tongue tied. How should I know? It's so hard to decide. I'm just trying to keep today all together. "Later on" is beyond my scope of interest.

This youth group is the first place I've been able to keep any friends. That's supposedly another LD problem. My school friends either treat me like a dummy or they drop me after awhile. I really get afraid of making new friends. The kids here seem to treat me pretty well.

I'm sort of coming back to church. I used to love Sunday School as a kid — all of the songs, the stories about Jesus, the coloring and projects, and the take-home papers. But some of my teachers didn't know how to handle me. Mom and Dad got embarrassed a few times when teachers would pull them out of church to come and get me. I wasn't trying to be bad. I would just get jittery and want to do something else. As I got older and we did more book study and writing, I started to feel like I always did at school — a big idiot. I quit going.

I like the youth group games and the short lessons and our activities. Then I feel like I'm equal to everyone else. That's a new feeling and I love it. Thank you for tracking me down and encouraging me to come back and try youth group. It's becoming the bright spot of my life.

But don't let the other kids know that I'm LD. They might not let me hang around anymore.

Being Bright and Feeling Simple-Minded

Welcome to Bryan's world. It's a world of deflated self-esteem, survival tactics, and embarrassment. It's full of confusion, misunderstanding, frustration, and guilt. The Bryans forget simple things and find learning the biggest barrier of all. They get a tight pit in their stomachs every day as they walk the school halls to their classrooms. They become emotionally numb and live in fear of being labeled *stupid*.

The learning disabled world is wrapped in the misconceptions of others. Misconceptions that equate learning disabilities as a form of retardation, which it is not. Or equating the LD child as a trouble-maker or below average. Misconceptions that interpret unruly behaviors as rebellion. Again, all untrue.

To be learning disabled means that learning is difficult under conventional means. It may mean that some of the processes involved in understanding or in using writing or speech in communication are somehow malfunctioning for the teenager. The ability to listen, think, speak, read, do math, spell, write, or converse logically may not be working correctly. It is not a problem of intelligence, desire, or intention. It is a problem of not being able to learn.

More specific terms used to describe learning disabilities include such conditions as dyslexia, developmental aphasia, brain dysfunction, Attention Deficit-Hyperactivity Disorder, and perceptual handicaps. While volumes have been written on these and other learning disabilities, it is enough for our purposes to realize that this is a huge field of inquiry. These kids are in our groups and need our help. They are victims of their disabilities and need us to encourage them, make room for them, work with them, and show them a loving Christ. We never want their learning about Christ to be disabled.

Some Common Characteristics

It used to be thought that just a few thousand children, nationwide, had learning disability problems. This number was thought to be so few, in fact, that little was done to help them or to research the problems of these youth extensively. As a result, millions of children struggled through their school years unaided.

Now it is well accepted that millions of children, from elementary school through college, struggle with learning disabilities. Laws have been enacted which insure that these kids get help. Things are slowly changing.

Be assured, you have kids in your youth group troubled by learning disabilities. The brighter the kid, the better he or she will be able to hide or compensate for the disability. They are remarkable in that they internally adjust and rearrange information so it makes sense. Here are some clues about LD teenagers:

—Often average or above-average in intelligence yet perform below their tested ability levels.

—Often unable to master some basic aspects of skills like math, reading, and language.

—May show difficulty in discriminating between some sounds, even though hearing tests show that hearing is normal. Also, may not be able to follow orally given instructions, remember what is heard, or be able to "screen" out unnecessary sounds or noise distractions.

—The same inability to discriminate may affect eyesight. Eye tests may be normal but reading may be scrambled, letters inverted, or the teen may not be able to distinguish between some objects.

—The kids become frustrated by their difficulties and develop poor self-images.

—LD teenagers often compensate by becoming behavior problems at school, at home, socially, and at church.

—They cannot recall what has been taught on a day-to-day basis.

—They may copy incorrectly. What is seen may be very different from what is copied.

—Many cannot tell a story in proper sequence.

—Often LD teenagers struggle with speaking English that is grammatically correct.

—Time management and starting or completing tasks is difficult.

—They tend to avoid assignments and chores, fearful that they won't be able to do them correctly.

—They may be hyperactive or excessively slow.

—They can lack motivation, be poor at self-control, and avoid following through.

—It is difficult, if not impossible for these teenagers, to categorize, classify, or order information. Some cannot distinguish between fact and fiction.

—Memory may be a problem, as well as attention and doing projects that require building or "putting together" skills.

—Some cannot think abstractly and hold to the literal, concrete understanding.

—It is extremely easy to distract these kids, and they find it impossible to sit very long with any activity.

Not all LD kids have all of these characteristics. These disabilities will range between severe to mild. But, no matter what the disorder or how bad they have it, LD kids will fear any youth group that is run too much like school. As leaders, we can learn how to reach them effectively with a little variation in our programs.

Ramifications for Our Youth Programs

After reading the above characteristics, we have to face the fact that Christianity may be somewhat troublesome for these kids. When we talk of Jesus living in our hearts, we are dealing with an abstract theological idea. While most children and teenagers can grasp the idea that this a spiritual presence, a learning disabled teenager may need some help to develop an understanding of the concept. The same will be true with presentations on aspects of the Holy Spirit, the significance of baptism or the Lord's Supper, and studies about God. Because we speak of spiritual, invisible, eternal things so often in presenting our faith, we may need to build these truths in very small steps.

This is not to say that children with learning difficulties cannot accept Christ or make poor Christians. Nothing could be farther from the truth. It only means that we, as leaders, need to offer literal, concrete explanations, whenever possible, as we present the more abstract aspects of our faith.

The larger ramification to a youth group is that LD kids, by high school, may feel like outsiders or failures. They need little reason to drop out when the program gets too challenging. When things don't make sense, the LD teenager, to save face, may simply disappear.

Over the years, I have seen this happen several times. Kids suddenly get "too busy" or "no longer interested" in youth group. Careful and courteous probing may reveal that the truth is that Jane or Jim feel lost. I often hear, "everyone knows more about the Bible than me," or "the other kids can follow and participate but I'm clueless." Recently, this happened in my group with a longtime member. He could no longer live the charade of what he perceived as his ignorance. Yet, it wasn't ignorance. His learning was met with many difficulties and barriers.

So what helps? The glorious truth is that aid is often extremely simple. I find that mentoring, or a one-on-one relationship of matching the teenager with an advisor, works wonders. Someone who can take the extra few minutes to break the information down, answer the questions, and encourage the teenager. These kids are rarely dumb; they just learn differently or learning is difficult.

I once was a pen pal with a fellow who needed help in grasping aspects of our faith. He was not cynical, not antagonistic to the faith, and not a critic. He just could not grasp the lesson in the lecture, read it from the Bible, talk in small groups, and ask questions in the format that we used so often. However, he could understand it if I wrote it to him.

For quite sometime we would write back and forth as he questioned the parts he had trouble understanding. When he saw it in print, he could work through it in such a way that he could understand. It took lots of time, but the young man is a solid believer and a wonderful brother in Christ.

In the Learning Disabilities literature such an innovation is often referred to as an Individualized Education Program. In other words, it is a matter of finding out what works for the teenager and meeting him or her on ground comfortable for them. This is imperative for the more than 2 million LD kids in our midst.

Finding out what works can be accomplished by involving parents and, ultimately, the schools which your LD kids attend. As part of your parent meetings or mailings to parents, mention that you are concerned about kids in the group who have any type of learning disability. Suggest that parents contact you personally so you can form a plan for spiritual education which meets the learning difficulties of their children. Most of the time parents will respond with deep appreciation.

Parents will usually be able to connect you with the LD teacher at the schools where their kids attend. This person is often grateful and amazed that you, the youth leader, are willing to work at including the LD teenager. With this network of parents, teacher, and you working to develop a plan of inclusive ministry, it is very unlikely that the teenagers with learning difficulties will leave the group. Church becomes a haven of acceptance and understanding.

Problem Kids

Something must be said about the learning disabilities that tend toward disruptive behavior. Attention Deficit-Hyperactivity Disorder (ADHD) is a controversial disorder that is hotly debated by educational and psychological professionals. Is it a learning disability or is it another type of disorder? The vote is still out. However, it is certain that these kids often have learning troubles. Studies show that ADHD kids experience problems in:

- language or memory deficits
- impaired ability to grasp concepts or develop perception
- difficulty in controlling their attention
- low impulse control

These kids, when tested, often have average to above average intelligence. They are not dumb! They simply do not adapt and integrate learning as one would expect.

Additionally, these kids know how to turn the pot up to boiling. On an extended trip, these kids bounce off the walls of the bus. During a longer lesson or

Bible study these kids fidget, talk, crack jokes, walk about the room, and generally disrupt. As one youth worker put it, ADHD teenagers are the ones he most often "wants to choke." Yet, they need our love and help.

Studies show that ADHD and learning disabilities frequently share the same symptoms. Rather than treating these kids as your "pet problems," it may be mutually beneficial to offer them behavior alternatives during activities which may be almost impossible for them to endure.

Helps for Learning Disabled Teenagers

The following suggestions are generally regarded as helps for learning disabled kids. More specific helps for more specific problems can be discovered through researching particular disabilities found among your kids. The library or the school guidance/learning disabilities counselor may be able to help you.

• During study programs, give all of the kids a detailed course syllabus of what lessons will be covered on what week. Perhaps you could include major topics and verses. This enables the LD kids to prepare for the study.

• Spell out expectations of any activity. The rules, the itinerary, what will be accomplished, etc. This allows the LD kids to prepare mentally and emotionally for the experience.

• During teaching times, use visual aids, such as outlines or writing on the board, to reinforce the lesson. It is also helpful to pick a couple of key points and repeat them over and over as part of the lesson. These become anchors for the teenager.

• Reinforce any theological terms with handouts. For example, all of the kids will benefit from definitions in language they can understand when dealing with special words like redemption, grace, justification, sanctification, and the like.

• Develop lessons that have a strong oral presentation, with lots of movement, hand gestures, and other expressions, as well as a reinforcing written section. Brief study sheets can be easily developed and reproduced for almost any lesson.

• Make questions and answers a major part of any experience. While natural during lessons, Q's and A's are also wonderful reinforcements during mission trips or other activities, after a sermon or special speaker, and when the group is sitting around. Treat all questions with integrity. LD kids get the message fast when questions are seen as a hassle by leaders.

• Choices and decisions can be nightmares for LD kids, so make yourself available as a sounding board. However, avoid giving advice. Don't make the decisions for the kids. They have to live the results.

• Be willing to repeat directions as often as needed. LD kids will need to check and recheck to make sure they are on track. Don't become frustrated or irritated. They will pick it up and quit asking. That's when the problems begin.

• Work as simply as possible. LD kids get confused with too many symbols. Slowly and simply are great rules. Again, mentors make good interpreters for the LD teenager.

• Allow some extra space for LD kids. It takes them additional time to "get in the groove" of any activity or lesson. If you rush them along or overlook their needs, they either bottle up and stuff their frustrations inside, or they blow up, spreading their anger over the entire group. Let them have some freedom to do what they need to do. Most often they won't act out inappropriately. Their actions usually are just what they need.

• Avoid time pressure activities. LD kids function under a different pace. The pressure will be unendurable.

• Remember that frustration is a reality for these kids. They can become frustrated at the smallest thing. When you sense frustration building, slow down or pull them aside and help them through it. Many unpleasant scenes can be avoided through an extra moment. Again, a mentor here works wonders.

• Be brave enough to admit when you don't know something. It is better to say, "I don't know. Let's try to find the answer to that together." Now you become an ally. In admitting to the gaps in your own knowledge and experience, you teach that learning is sometimes difficult for everyone, but answers are often obtainable through a little work. This example will help everyone, not just the LD teen.

Science is still trying to figure out why the information gets scrambled between the senses and the brains of the learning disabled. Yet, this disadvantage can be overcome, to some degree, with caring, acceptance, and some extra attention.

Sometimes love is spelled **t-i-m-e**. Sometimes it is spelled **u-n-d-e-r-s-t-a-n-d-i-n-g**. For the learning disabled teenager, your efforts will mean more than you will ever know. Your youth program will become an oasis to them. And Jesus becomes a very special Friend because He loved them so much He sent them you.

Programming Ideas

For You:

1. As suggested, get in touch with parents, school teachers to the learning disabled, community

specialists, and library resources to broaden your basic knowledge of learning disabilities. Find out which kids in your group struggle with which problems. Before you can make a difference you must know the size and specifics of the problem.

2. Develop some training sheets and resources about learning difficulties for use with your advisors. These are also helpful in church camp or retreat settings. At such times counselors can be quickly trained to minimize the frustrating situations that seem to set off LD kids. Share what you are learning.

3. Occasionally spend a few minutes reflecting on what it would be like to have learning disabilities. Try to feel the confusion, frustration, and rejection. Imagine what it would be like to be classified as dumb when you know that you are smart. Use these feelings to nurture your compassion and understanding of the LD kids in your group.

4. If you have a learning disability, reflect on how you felt as a teen. How do you feel now? Again, this is useful material as you reach out to others.

For the Learning Disabled Teenagers:

1. Talk to them! Let them know that you realize they struggle at times. Ask them how you can help.

Usually by high school the teenagers have a pretty good grasp on their learning limitations. They may be able to tell you lots of helpful things.

I often find that high school LD kids have developed some alternate means for learning. Some rearrange the material in a fashion that makes it understandable to them. One clue is the teenager who takes notes on scraps of paper during lessons and pockets them. Later they will process what was taught into their own "learning language." Ask them about it.

2. Develop study sheets, clear itineraries, program or study syllabi, weekly program schedules with all of the details outlined, rules, expectations, etc. in printed form. Make it a habit. Don't see it as a hassle. This is the easiest way to communicate to the families of the LD teenagers, as well as the kids themselves. If these materials are in print, parents, friends, and mentors can walk the LD kids through them at the speed that best suits them. Remember, a slow learning speed does not imply intellectual dullness.

3. Explore the possibilities of a mentoring program for the kids. "Disguise" these volunteers as youth advisors. Often we divide our teenagers among our advisors to insure all of the kids get regular contact from a leader. Give mentors fewer kids and specially train them to help LD kids. These special friends become interpreters of lessons, directions, and programs. They can follow up when more abstract lessons are taught to make sure the LD teenager understood what was taught.

4. Many colleges now have programs for LD kids. They can be encouraged to seek further education. For many this will be an exciting, but scary, possibility.

Special helps, learning aids, tutors, understanding teachers, and more will greet the LD student who studies at a college or university which is sensitive to the needs of the learning disabled. Here, again, you give hope.

For the Whole Group:
1. Openly discuss learning disabilities from the point that all of us have strengths and weaknesses. Encourage each person to admit to their intellectual challenges or shortcomings. Whether math or

language arts, literature or wood shop, art class or cooking, we all have areas where the information does not quite sink in. Sharing the problem makes the specific problems of LD kids less funny or peculiar. When we all share a problem, we are less likely to ridicule another for it.

2. Invite teachers of learning disabled teens in to explain what life is like for these kids. Again, springboard from the point that we all have limitations. Learning disabilities are much like physical coordination. There are many different levels of competency. Older kids tend to accept this in sports. A Christian LD expert coming in can help them grasp that about learning.

3. Equalize the group through the use of study sheets and other printed resources, as well as using the suggested communications tips mentioned above. All of the kids will benefit from your more careful distribution of information. So will their families. Do not present these approaches just for LD kids!

Ministering to LD kids is a wonderful expression of the compassion of Christ. It sends the message that all are wanted and welcome in your youth group. Your ministry to all of the kids helps them to realize that none of us are perfect, and we all need the acceptance and understanding of each other.

Your youth group can become a special haven to the LD teenagers. It takes a little work to initiate, but the dividends in the lives of the kids and their response to your ministry is life-changing. Ministry should make a difference. This is one difference your LD kids will appreciate.

10/ The Physically Handicapped Teenager

Tara's Story

Moving to a new community also meant finding a new church. My old church was so perfect. A new church was scary to me.

When we visited this church for the first time, I noticed an invitation in the bulletin directed at new kids. It was a welcome to visit the youth group that evening. Mom suggested I try it.

I wasn't too sure, but as we left the worship service a wonderful thing happened. Two girls who attended the youth group approached me, introduced themselves, and personally invited me to the evening's meeting. Their warmth and sincerity hooked me, and I agreed to return that evening.

I was so excited! All day long I looked forward to that meeting. It was to be some kind of "Mystery Fun Nite." The only clue given was that we were advised to wear casual, grubby clothing. It was so irresistible!

As I arrived at the church that evening and entered the lobby, I felt that attending this church wouldn't be so bad. I started believing that I had found a new youth group "home." Then, as the youth leaders began to explain the evening's activity, I knew this group wasn't going to work. My heart fell.

The group was going on a mystery hike through the wooded property next to the church. We were to divide into teams, follow clues through the woods, and race to see which group could find the secret rendezvous first. While this game sounds wonderful, it is impossible for a person in a wheelchair.

As they began picking teams, I wheeled out the back and went to find a place to cry. The saddest part was that I could see the relief on the faces of some of the kids as I "snuck" away. Even the two girls who had invited me looked relieved. They weren't to blame, I know. They couldn't have known what the mystery activity was, or they wouldn't have invited me in the first place.

I hid, the teams left, and no one even noticed me. Stuff like this happens to me all the time. But I'm not going back to that church.

My old church was cool. When I had the accident, they re-thought the structure and what the youth pastor called the "meaning" of youth group. He believed the youth program should include all of the kids. I have discovered since this move that he is a rarity.

I still have my faith. I still have my family. I still have my own devotional life with Christ. But I don't think I'll find a church. It hurts too much to try.

The Excluded World of the Handicapped

I once witnessed a college experiment in which the students participated in a handicapped awareness program. Each person drew a partner for the weekend project. One partner was designated as a healthy, physically intact person. The other was asked to draw from a box which contained cards describing various physical handicaps. The handicaps included blindness, loss of use of legs or arms, deafness, paralysis, and other difficulties. The retreat was to help students experience what life is like for handicapped persons.

The most interesting segment of the retreat was when the group descended on a local restaurant for Sunday breakfast. This was the first major excursion away from the retreat site. By this time the non-handicapped persons had learned to aid their partners appropriately without doing everything for them. The designated handicapped folks had learned that the world is most often a barrier. Each participant was immediately aware, upon entering the restaurant, that others treat the handicapped as if blindness or paralysis were contagious.

In the debriefing following the retreat, the overwhelming response by the participants was that they did not know life was so hard for those with physical limitations. They were shocked to discover that many businesses, schools, churches, and public facilities, like parks and some museums, made it difficult for those with limitations to participate.

Finally, they were astounded at the "reception" the handicapped received, through stares, unkind remarks, and patronizing. This group felt enriched as a result of the experience. They had tasted the world of the 88 million handicapped or disabled Americans.

I have too often been like the youth leaders in Tara's story. In my zeal to provide a varied and interesting program, I forgot that the participants come in all kinds of packages. While we rarely find the perfect activity that allows for the needs of all, we can provide fewer programs which focus upon the abilities of a few. I am not as concerned with being "fair," for life is rarely based upon fairness, as I am with making sure Christianity isn't only for the perfectly healthy.

The world of the handicapped is often a lonely world of exclusion and limitation. It is plagued by barriers, misunderstanding, and stares. The terrible reality is that this need not be so.

With a bit of insight and thoughtfulness, the church's youth program can incorporate almost any handicapped teenager. In fact, a 1991 study showed changes costing as little as $50.00 could make accessibility a reality for 50% of the nation's handicapped. As a rule of thumb, if the teenager can get to the meeting without the threat of harm, there are ways to include him or her in the program most of the time.

Breaking Stereotypes

Before entering into ministry with teenagers having handicaps, the first area of change must be within us, as leaders. We must not view handicapped kids as handicapped. It does teenagers with physically-based limitations little good to have us, as leaders, perpetuating the myth that they can't participate.

One way to think differently about those with physical limitations is to use a different term in your thinking. New terms being used are helpful in breaking the mentality of limitation. Instead of disabled, some prefer "other-abled" or "physically challenged." These terms raise the focus from what the person can't do to other ways of participating — the "other" approach. This Other Approach looks for alternatives to accomplish the same goal.

For example, other-abled teenagers love to play games — high activity, exciting games. What about Capture the Flag? Too fast? Too rough? Too limiting? Then you've never seen a jailer in a wheelchair. She or he will defend the inmates as well as anyone. Sure, they may not be able to run over hill and dale seeking out the flag, but each team needs members playing in different capacities anyway. Our friend, Tara, would much rather play jailer than stay home.

Assess the obvious limitations of the other-abled in your group and come up with inclusive alternatives. This makes a strong statement that any teenagers can participate in the church and your programs.

It is important to remember, strange as it may sound, that physical problems, from the most severe to the least, are not to be equated with mental illness or retardation. Talk to your handicapped kids about their perceptions of the group, activities, and their involvement. Learn their stories and their experiences due to the handicap. They'll tell you stories like people talking about them as if they were not there. People pointing, staring, and laughing at them. Folks being rude, bothersome, or inquisitive. Allow other-abled teenagers the opportunity to keep their self-respect and integrity. This can be done by letting them talk.

Physically limiting problems come in all varieties. From the inability to walk or use arms or hands, to not being able to hear, see, or talk. The manifestation of the inability is not as problematic as the attitudes we may have. Too often we determine that other-abled teenagers can or cannot do something without consulting them.

I had a young woman in my youth group who frequently had seizures and walked with a severe limp. She was a vibrant person and extremely active in youth group and life. As I began my ministry with that church, I quickly discovered that Carol was not going to be left out even though she had some limitation. We all wanted her to be part of the group, so it was important to discover the extent to which she would be limited in participation. I decided to meet with her mother.

I was amazed to learn that Carol could do it all: sports, action games, hikes, whatever. She would be slower, but she could run.

The most serious issue was when she had a seizure. They could not be predicted. Rather than not allow her to attend our functions, we all learned how to care for her when a seizure occurred. With her withered arm and dragging leg, Carol played baseball, soccer, canoed, and joyously worshiped God. Since we didn't limit her, she learned not to limit herself. She would occasionally have a seizure, but we sat with her, cradled her head in our laps, and loved her through them.

Jesus and Physical Handicaps

Physical difficulties were not unknown in Jesus' world. The Bible is rich in lessons about those with physical difficulties. We remember Jesus feuding with the Pharisees (Matthew 12:1-14) about healing the lame or disfigured on the Sabbath. The Son of God maintained the value and quality of human life in the face of rules and provided relief to the hurting.

Sadly, many of our church youth groups have unwritten rules which exclude physically limited teenagers.

The Bible records over 120 instances that include such handicaps as blindness, crippling conditions, and various disabilities. Few argue that the handicapped are not fully acceptable within God's family. Yet, we limit their participation. Catch 22.

Jesus loves all and ministers to all. As His ambassadors, we need to re-think ways in which we limit others made by our Creator and make any necessary changes.

Recently, a church asked me to help them determine the kinds of adjustments that would be needed to allow all of their youth to participate in church functions. Having no elevator, it was obvious that the first and easiest adjustment would be to relocate the youth rooms to the ground floor. Although this was the most inexpensive solution, they fell prey to the "it has never been done that way before" disease and decided against the change.

It was soon obvious that this church did not seriously intend to make the youth programs available to all. They were only discussing changes theoretically.

When funds are not available to make the best of all worlds for the kids who are limited, turn to fresh ideas and approaches. The restriction that is greater than physical, mental, or situational limitations is within our own minds. I firmly believe that almost any teenager can participate in the youth group in some reasonable, satisfying level.

Sometimes a teenager comes to us who is so horribly disfigured or handicapped that only a limited level of participation is possible. Talk to them and you'll find they are willing to be a cheerleader or scorekeeper when it is impossible to play the game. They delight in being with the group and a part of the group. It is far more satisfying than being alienated and alone. The challenge to us in leadership is to reciprocate appropriately and plan activities that can fully include them just as they are.

The gift each of us offers to others is our presence. Our other-abled teenagers are a gift, just as they are. They need our love and acceptance as they travel their own journey in Christ, just as the fully able do. They need example and guidance. Just as the fully able do. They occasionally need the services of our counseling skills and listening ears. They need to bounce ideas off of us. They need to be in the group as a member, fully accepted. Isn't it wonderfully strange that their needs are exactly the same as every other group member!

Programming Ideas

For You:

1. Take some time to learn about physical handicaps. While the physical symptoms are important, a knowledge of the psychological impact of being disabled is essential. These kids often need to be drawn out, so you need an understanding of life from their point of view. Some research on your part will be time well spent.

2. Spend some time talking to those with handicaps. Note the differences in the experiences of those who were handicapped from birth and those who received an injury which disabled them. Listen for their views on becoming other-abled. How did they adjust? Did they reclaim their lives? What obstacles did they face?

It is also helpful to talk to someone who has not recovered in a healthy fashion. Such hurting people can make the dynamics of being disabled shockingly clear. Not all regain their lives. For some, the handicap overwhelms them.

As effective leaders, we need to understand their stories. This will help us to encourage our other-abled youth through their adjustment times. Stories of pain reveal things we would rather not hear. Yet they are stories we need to hear.

3. Assign yourself a handicap from time to time. I have blindfolded myself to experience life as a blind person. I have walked on crutches. I have tried to get around in my church in a wheelchair, experiencing the limitations. The awareness is astounding.

From this kind of awareness, role play inside yourself how such frustrations would feel day in and day out. Let your imagination run with it. How would your life be limited? What would you miss? Consider such areas as dating, your ability to shop, and visits to the homes of your friends. Realizing these are the same feelings and experiences your disabled teenagers face daily will be sobering. Use these revelations to make appropriate adjustments in your youth program.

4. Ask your church trustees or leaders to assess the limiting factors with your church properties. Someone has to "lead the charge" if change is going to come.

5. It is possible that some handicapped teenagers have already fallen through the cracks. They may have been programmed out of the church. If you are new, you may not know these kids exist.

Ask around and gather names. Then, go see these kids. Talk to them honestly about their handicap. Discuss what it would take to allow them to participate in youth activities. Talk about the church facilities. Open up the area of attitudes, painful remarks, and the like. Do not make promises you may not be able to keep. Simply gather information.

Armed with this data, meet with other youth advisors, leaders, and sponsors. Discuss how the youth program can be expanded to include these other-abled kids. Suggest some of them go and visit the more open kids. Open communication is the foundation upon which this expansion of ministry may grow.

For the Other-Abled Teenagers:
1. Those having difficulty getting out or around will benefit from regular visits from you, other advisors, and the youth. Handicapped teenagers are not exempt from loneliness. The first step in beginning a ministry for the other-abled is contacting them and developing trust. Once you and other advisors have done this, get your teenagers involved.

Initially, you'll want to accompany them as they visit the home bound or alienated teenagers. While the kids may be open to the concept of visiting the disabled, they may not be ready for the shock if the teenager is especially deformed. Don't protect, but fully inform. Once the bridge of the first visit has been crossed and the relationship is established, the teenagers will do fine. Love overcomes the outside and discovers the person within.

2. A support group for the handicapped can be a great aid. Meetings can focus upon the frustrations these kids face daily. They desperately need a vent.

Families often need ministry, too. The guilt that a "normal" child feels when his or her sibling is disabled is often overwhelming. These captives can be set free. While such supports can be extremely therapeutic, do not pretend to offer help if you are not trained to do so. Seek out a professional to help the group. Talking, listening, and establishing relationships is the focus of such support groups, not advice or problem solving.

It is not uncommon for this kind of ministry to be a great evangelism tool for the church. Hurting people are searching for churches who accept them in their pain and offer something to counter it.

3. Many communities offer established programs for physically challenged persons. Investigate these programs and plug into them as you feel appropriate. Your ability to provide networking to needy families or teenagers will be greatly enhanced through such associations, as will your knowledge of handicaps in general.

4. Learn to call ahead to check out any place where you may have an activity. Shops, camps, retreat centers, universities, sporting events — each location needs to be investigated for barriers. If you neglect to do so, you may find that you are unable to treat the handicapped teenager with the respect they deserve.

We once had a teenager in a heavy, motorized wheelchair attend a function at another church with our group. Upon arriving we found the rally was to be held in a gym on the second floor. We assumed that it would be no problem to carry the person, wheelchair and all, up the stairs. We got her up the steps with no problem, but it was done at the expense of the young woman's self-respect.

Think what it would feel like to have four big guys surround you, grab your chair, lift you, and lug you up a flight of stairs with the rest of your youth group following. I'd be humiliated as an adult. Think of the reaction a teenager would likely have. What teenager is going to want that much attention over a disability? Such treatment is less than loving.

Especially when one phone call would have given the teenager foreknowledge and a choice.

There is increased awareness today concerning the needs of handicapped persons in our country. But many barriers still need to come down. Your calls and inquiries help raise accessibility issues with those in charge of the facilities you visit.

5. Begin a program in which the other-abled teenager is introduced to new skills and experiences. Depending on the type of disability, there are aids for such activities as painting, writing, computer work, and other interests. Handicapped should never imply that life stops short! There are still too many discoveries to be made!

Visit a physical therapist for ideas especially matched to particular handicaps. Physical therapists can be found in hospitals, schools, and in private practice. Often they will be willing to volunteer time to help teenagers adjust.

For the Entire Group:

1. Rent a Joni Eareckson Tada movie and experience this touching story of how one young woman with a life of unbound promise suddenly finds herself paralyzed from the neck down. Yet, with the love and power of Jesus Christ, she discovers a whole new life of service to God and others. Her books are inspirational and challenging; her story is dynamite. The books and movies will be a stretching experience for all the youth.

2. Begin a sponsorship program of physically-challenged teenagers. Match them with an adult or teenager. It is almost impossible to simply "take" a handicapped teenager to an amusement park, some museums, a concert, etc. as one of the group.

However, a one-on-one sponsorship/friendship match makes this possible.

The drawback can be that some non-handicapped teenagers are uncomfortable or too self-centered for this. They will think this relationship cramps their day. While it can be novel for awhile, the first time Joe or Jane misses the roller coaster because they are sharing the day with a handicapped friend, the whole relationship is tested. Some kids will grumble; others will be fine.

Sponsorship programs are not for every teenager. Yet, they are valuable enough to try. Even the teenager who tries it and drops out will develop a higher appreciation for what it is like being handicapped.

3. Use such temporary handicaps as a broken limb, a brief hospital stay, or an operation as learning experiences. If your youth group opens its doors and hearts to other-abled teenagers, open and honest discussions will be allowed. An injury can open the door to great talks about handicaps, life-long disability, and similar topics.

4. Rather than attending a "regular" camp that may have some handicap accessibility for your next retreat, book it at a camp that is designed for handicapped use entirely. Turn the tables and challenge the non-handicapped kids to "fit in" for a change rather than the physically challenged kids adapting. This is not a punishment or an attempt to be fair. It is another way in which consciousness can be raised. It will be a great relief for the other-abled teenagers to be on more comfortable turf.

5. Design a retreat experience similar to the one described earlier in which certain teenagers adopt a handicap for a weekend and another teenager acts as his or her sponsor. While the sky is the limit, I think

it is important to make at least one public appearance in a restaurant. The stares, the unkind remarks, the barriers are all more effective than a thousand lectures or speakers.

6. Swimming and horseback riding are two activities which many handicapped persons can enjoy with little risk. Planning these recreational activities make for a great day for all the kids. Call ahead and make sure that the facility is aware that other-abled teenagers will be in your party and describe their limitations in detail. This helps prepare a wonderful day for the whole group.

7. Encourage open communication between all specialized groups within the youth group. This kind of interchange helps the entire group learn how they can live together with respect for each one's personal limitations and difficulties.

It is both heart rending and challenging to hear the stories of other-abled teenagers. The shattered dreams, the hopes and fears, the wondering about love and marriage, the disappointment with God. Yet, there is also the sense of what they have learned, the new person they have become, and how they realize the presence of God. Be prepared for moments of tears, bitterness, and frustration. Don't try to cover these emotional responses with some platitude. Let the kids tell their stories.

As the leader, you may want to have some questions prepared which are respectful but probe deeper into the ways life is different. "What big differences do you see?" "What attitudes are most hurtful?" "What fears do you have?" "What should non-handicapped people know about your particular disability?" Try to imagine what questions the non-handicapped kids might like to have discussed, but will be afraid to ask.

8. Do a series of Bible studies on the difficult topic of healing. Tackle this issue with openness and let the kids ask what my group calls the "Big Q's" — those questions that seem to be unanswerable but need to be asked.

I heard a study given by a blind minister which was life changing for me. This man, although blind, believed in God's ability to use him completely. His talk sparked in me the idea that handicapped kids can and do fit into our youth programs.

9. Put other-abled kids on the planning group within your program. Let them choose for themselves which activities they wish to sponsor. Don't decide for them which ones are more "appropriate." You may limit them. They will act wisely and responsibly if given the space and the respect inherent in this approach.

Sometimes other-abled kids will participate in planning an activity that they know they cannot do. This may be their means of service to others. It is like anyone in leadership. You find you can't do it all. This is no different for our other-abled kids.

Sometimes physical limitations make it easy for us to overlook those who have them. Consciously or unconsciously, we exclude them as part of our youth groups. Adding these kids and making them part of the core of your group is a delight to them and a great pleasure to our Lord who gave Himself for each one. Your ministry will change lives when you open it to all.

11/ Teenagers with Eating Disorders

Suzi's Story

When I look in the mirror, the "me" that I see is not the real "me." At least that's what my counselor says.

I see a body totally out of whack. My legs are chunky; my stomach is massive, and my face is fat. I want to diet even more. How did I get so heavy?

My counselor says I have a "body image distortion." She says this means I somehow distort the way I view myself. She wants me to believe that I'm not heavy at all. She shows me medical charts on normal weight and height for my age, but I know that chart is wrong. My body is different. How can she say I'm 20 pounds underweight when I am obviously obese?

My counselor always tries to find out what's going on at home. That really bugs me. What does my family have to do with me being fat? She says that my disorder, anorexia nervosa, can be related to what she calls "control issues." She believes that my distorted body image is linked to a feeling I have that my life is out of control.

I think she's wrong, but I have to admit that life is too fast for me. Dad gets transferred about every 18 months. We pack and move, pack and move. I've learned some short cuts like only unpacking what I need and staying to myself. At the last move I didn't join the youth group at our new church. And that used to be my favorite thing. But why bother?

Life goes on. I'd maybe listen to the counselor more if I thought it would do any good. She might be a little right. But then it hits me. We won't be living here much longer, so what's the use?

Scott's Story

The trouble with people is that they won't leave others alone. They love to meddle and tell you how to live your life. Do they think I'm stupid? How about that school counselor who asked me if I knew that I was overweight? I was speechless! Do I know that I'm overweight?! Everyday of my miserable life someone makes it their personal duty to remind me. They are exceeded in their unkindness only by their creativity in finding new names to call me.

Even at youth group I get an occasional rude remark. But, at least there I believe that the kids are trying. The new youth pastor, Jake, has had lots to do with that and I admit I'm feeling a new acceptance. He sometimes talks about his weight problems, too. He knows that I'm not going to change through intimidation or shame. This guy really accepts me for who I am.

Once he told me that things could be different if I wanted to try. "Great," I thought, "another adult with a new diet for me to try." Then I realized that he wasn't talking about my weight. He was talking about me. What a shock.

We talked about how things could be different. Jake said that sharing our problems with a good Christian friend and praying really help. I became a Christian in the fifth grade so I knew what he was talking about. But I also knew that my church seemed to be embarrassed by me. Somehow I knew I could trust Jake to be that friend I needed.

We began meeting to talk and pray and just be pals. Jake was great because he didn't stop with my body fat. He was also concerned about what was going on inside me. He knew that my pain was real and deeply entrenched. Jake soon figured out that I was starving for love and trying to fill it by shoveling food into the void.

My family has always missed the real me. Mom and Dad love me, but they haven't told me or shown me in years. No hugs, no kisses, no compliments, nothing.

To compensate, I learned that food can make me feel better. When I feel bad, I eat. When I'm alone too long, I eat. When kids make fun of me, I eat. Food is always there for me and it never lets me down. Aside from God, food is the only thing that makes me feel complete.

Jake understands this, but he hasn't suggested that I stop eating. He says that we might be able to find ways to fill my "love void" through church, other ministries, and the youth group so that I won't need the food substitute. I'm getting excited about working with Jake. I don't want to be fat and repulsive to others. I want to be loved.

Thin as an Obsession
We are a society that prizes the slim and trim. We worship health, fitness, and exercise and scorn those who follow a more sedentary lifestyle. While there is

nothing wrong with healthy living, there is something wrong with the message that humans are better if they are eternally young, tanned all year long, and firmly fit. This is strongly communicated to our teenagers and reinforced in almost every media outlet.

Teen magazines, shows aimed at teenaged audiences, and products marketed for teenagers always use "beautiful people" as their marketing images. No wrinkles, no extra body fat, no flabby muscles, perfect hair, and so on convey the message that average is less than desirable. When girls with perfect bodies clad in skimpy bathing suits are used to sell chewing gum, we should know we're in trouble.

Teenagers with eating disorders have seen these messages and believe them. The lean look, the together appearance, and the healthy build either become a compulsion, in that they feel a need to become more skinny, or a reinforcement that their already overweight, out-of-shape body is a waste. These teenagers are crying inside.

The Eating Disorders

Eating disorders are extremely difficult to treat. Unlike other substance-related problems in which the substance may be eliminated to begin recovery, eating disorders are related to something we all need to survive — food. We can't tell a person who has an eating disorder to stop eating. Special grace is needed to help teenagers who have eating disorders.

We'll look at three major eating disorders common today.

Anorexia nervosa. Teenagers become overwhelmed with a self-image of being "fat" and diet to the point of malnutrition and possible death.

Bulimia (sometimes called bulimia nervosa). The teenager eats large amounts of food in a short period of time (called binging or binge eating) and often follows this with self-induced purging through vomiting or taking laxatives.

Anorexia nervosa and bulimia are very real problems within our youth groups.

Obesity. Often overlooked as an eating disorder, the teenager uses food to compensate for something else. Overeating and being overweight are health hazards and are usually related to social and psychological difficulties in teenagers. While the risks of obesity may not be as immediately "deadly" as those above, the problems are very real. For this reason we add obesity to our ministry scope.

Pica. The person eats non-food substances like chalk, leaves, or pebbles. This is rare, however, being aware it exists is important.

Anorexia Nervosa

Anorexia nervosa is an emotional disorder characterized by a concern over weight and a preoccupation with food. The disorder can be deadly. It is sometimes called the "starvation sickness" or "dieter's disease" because anorexics refuse to eat. The name anorexia nervosa literally means "nervous loss of appetite," but this is inaccurate. Research shows that anorexics do feel hunger much of the time.

Anorexics suffer from a distorted belief that they are fat. They truly "see" excess fat when they look in the mirror. Facts have no bearing to the "reality" they perceive about their "overweight" bodies. Even when obviously underweight, anorexics fear becoming overweight and take starvation level measures to avoid any fat accumulation. The common complaint is that they "feel fat." Although males can be anorexic, about 90% of the known cases are among females.

Anorexia nervosa is most often found in middle to upper class teenagers. While black female adolescents are beginning to be reported, the huge majority are white. The fatality level of the disease is about 10%. Death usually occurs from complications from malnutrition. Those who do not die are often plagued with major physical, emotional, and psychological problems.

The increase of anorexia nervosa seems to correspond with a decrease in the so-called ideal weight for women over the last 20 years. This is typified by contestants in the Miss America pageant. Their average weight has decreased in the last 25 years. Meanwhile, the average weight of young women in our society has increased about 5 pounds. Our teenagers have noticed the changes. . .and the differences they see in their bodies.

Facts about Anorexia Nervosa:
- About 1 in every 100 to 150 girls becomes anorexic.
- Age of onset is usually after age 15. The age range is 12 to 20.
- A person is considered anorexic if their body weight is 15 to 25 percent below the average weight for their body type.
- Anorexics are likely to be depressed and report feeling a great deal of stress.
- About 500,000 people have been diagnosed as being anorexic and the figure is growing rapidly.

Major symptoms are: preoccupation with dieting and food, huge weight loss, excessive exercise, loss of ability to menstruate, wanting to be alone, mood swings, feelings of insecurity, and a feeling of helplessness and loneliness.

If the illness progresses, the person is likely to suffer physically and may incur permanent damage. Some tip offs are: lack of energy, pale skin, fatigue, dark and brittle nails, constipation, sensitivity to cold, hair loss, and reduced reaction time.

Anorexia nervosa is extremely difficult to treat, even by professionals. Our best investment, as youth workers, is to show love and support as "case managers" in bringing the teenager to help. Always refer this illness to professionals.

Recovery is possible. One study of 50 anorexics over a two year period found 86% continuing to recover.

Bulimia

Where anorexics will restrict food intake, those struggling with bulimia will wrestle with guilt about eating and eliminating the food through laxatives or self-induced vomiting. This "purging" is often preceded by "binge eating" in which large amounts of food are rapidly eaten in a short period of time. These foods are often extremely high in calories (1,200 to 11,500 calories per eating episode.)

Again, the plague of this eating disorder seems to be the self-concept of being "fat." Other characteristics include: a fear of not being able to stop eating, depression, self-criticism about eating behaviors, and poor adjustment to daily living.

Facts about Bulimia:

- Bulimics are overly concerned with weight reduction and usually are on some sort of diet or exercise program.

- The binging and purging will be irregular, not continuous.
- They can eat incredible amounts of food with almost double the regular calories of a normal meal.
- They may "hoard" or hide food.
- Often the foods are not healthy, such as eating shortening, sugar out of the bag, or large quantities of fast food or snacks.
- Bulimics may not have a routine meal schedule during a time that they are binging. They can binge and then not eat at all for a day or two.
- Some bulimics steal the food used in binging.
- Binging is usually followed by a time of self-criticism, stress, and, for some, intense exercise.

Bulimics, while predominantly female, can be found in any racial or ethnic group. The average age of involvement is high school through college age. There are some male bulimics, though, especially among athletic males.

In general, bulimics are overly impulsive, anxiety prone, depressed, hold a low self-image yet demand personal perfection, and possess a feeling of being unattractive. Many bulimics are extremely dependent upon others. Some 70% of those with bulimia report having suicidal thoughts following the binge-purge cycle.

Further clues of possible bulimic activity among your teenagers:
- Numerous trips to scales to check their weight.
- Increasing withdrawal from family, friends, school, and church functions.
- A pattern of secretive eating or only eating when alone.
- Reports or observations of vomiting following meals.
- Disappears after eating (may indicate vomiting).

- Excessive exercise.
- Denial of hunger.
- Abuse of laxatives, diuretics, or diet pills.
- Cuts or bruises on hands and knuckles from self-induced vomiting.
- If the teenager has been actively bulimic for some time, there may be an erosion of the dental enamel as a result of contact with stomach acids on the teeth from vomiting.
- Observing or hearing of eating inedible foods.

As with anorexia nervosa, the bulimic teenager must be referred to a professional counselor for help. Bulimics respond to treatment rather well, especially when involved in group counseling sessions. Family therapy is also helpful.

For both of these illnesses the consequences are very harmful physically, emotionally, psychologically, and spiritually. The body cannot take the self-induced abuses of these disorders for long periods of time without being harmed. Emotions are characterized by severe highs and lows. Mental health suffers to the point that many with these disorders desire suicide. Spiritually, these teenagers feel unacceptable to God while desperately wanting His love.

Obesity

Our society worships thin. Yet, moderate chubbiness is gaining ground as we watch the thin gods and goddesses of the TV screen while we chow down on snacks.

In general, we are becoming a heavier country. High school teenagers are said to be 5 to 7 pounds heavier than they were 20 years ago. Being a bit heavier is fine. However, for some the craving for food is a disease.

While most teenagers worry about their weight, only some 15% are truly obese. In these teenagers it is not a problem of a few extra pounds — it's lots of extra pounds. Additionally, other problems may emerge in sexual identity, dependency needs, peer relationships, and school performance.

Facts About Obesity:
There are three general causes for obesity:
- heredity, obesity tends to run in families.
- stress or crisis, some turn to food as a security.
- developmental issues, which arise from problems during the development of personality.

The outcome is a heavy, insecure, and hurting teenager desperately in need of our acceptance and care.

It is often assumed that heavy young people are extra big eaters. This may not be the case. Often, the obese teenager is a victim of poor nutrition. It has been noted that obese girls eat less food and less frequently than lean girls. The differences are in the nutritional value of the foods eaten and the amount of physical activity. Lean girls eat more food and more often, but they tend toward foods of better nutritional value and are physically active. Obese girls consume more calories than they burn through activity.

As with the other eating disorders, obesity is best left to medical or psychological treatment. Your role as friend and encouraging supporter will be an invaluable addition to the treatment plan.

In helping obese teenagers to regain control of their bodies, it is beneficial to understand the kinds of intervention techniques used by counselors. Many residential programs use a three dimensional emphasis of: 1) food and nutrition education, 2) a retraining of behaviors that may lead to overeating such as help with anger, depression, or social awkwardness, and 3) physical activity and exercise. These programs do work for the obese teenager. As Christians it is natural to add the love of Jesus and to encourage the young person in the relationship that they have with Him.

As Body People

A person once asked me why we even bother with such matters. He argued that we live this short life and then we go to be with the Lord, so why worry about our bodies? While I couldn't argue with his eternal hope, I did question his philosophy of life as a Christian. I believe that this life is a gift and should be lived with integrity before our loving God. If we don't help others along the way, we miss the core of the Good News.

God places us in bodies. They are remarkable, "fearfully and wonderfully made" (Psalm 139:14), to do His service (Romans 12:1). Jesus came to be among us in a human body to live life as we do. Not to care for our bodies is poor stewardship of the temple of God (I Corinthians 3:16).

Years ago a friend told me of a young woman in his youth group who was obese and had a severe case of acne. Terribly unattractive, she lived her life in the shadows of any social gathering. At church she was always there, but always alone. Life for "Lynda" was filled with pain, largely because of her appearance.

Eventually, the youth pastor took Lynda aside and said, "Lynda, I wonder if you have ever had a medical examination of your acne or received any suggestions about your weight problems?" Her look made him die a thousand deaths. Yet, after a few moments, she responded that she had not seen a doctor and did he think it might help? He said it wouldn't hurt to get checked out.

The happy ending is that Lynda did see a doctor and discovered that her acne could be treated. She began a program of diet and exercise, also under her doctor's care, and began to lose weight. Her self-image rose and her relationships with others improved dramatically. And, since her youth pastor cared enough to make the suggestion, her faith grew. She received a miracle of a whole new life both physically and spiritually. She was finally able to accept God's love.

Bodies come in all shapes and sizes. No two are alike. There is no standard body type, nor is one shape or size better than another. True, our society values certain looks over others. But that doesn't mean that the look is "better."

In ministering to teenagers with eating disorders, it is imperative that we not advocate our preferred body type. This can happen. Be careful of messages you may give.

If you feel that a teenager is struggling with an eating disorder, begin praying for guidance before taking any action. Talk to her or his parents and review the clues. To jump right in may damage the teenager and, with these kinds of problems, the teenager can compensate in negative ways. Remember, there is a severe self-image problem involved. Be careful not to add to the stress. Work with the family and the teenager to get him or her to see a doctor.

Programming Ideas
For You:
    1. Spend some time in the library at the

Periodical Index, then read some current articles on the various eating disorders. Many magazines focusing on health, teenagers, men and women's health issues, and related areas regularly publish articles on these issues. Reading a few will give you a good working knowledge on the most recent research, treatment, and new developments. Professional journals are also a good source of current information.

2. Current information and materials for your files are available through:

•National Association of Anorexia Nervosa and Associated Disorders, Box 7, Highland Park, IL, 60035.

•Anorexia Nervosa & Related Eating Disorders, Inc., Box 5102, Eugene, OR, 97405.

3. If possible, find someone with an eating disorder to talk to. Ask how it feels to struggle with these problems. It is hard to comprehend eating disorders if you have never had one. Talking to someone in recovery is illuminating and very helpful when trying to develop an understanding that can be used with teenagers.

Most recovering bulimics and anorexics will share their stories, field our questions, and correct our misconceptions. I learned much more by talking to a friend with bulimia than from all the research and reading I had done. And, these contacts become valuable in setting up a program for the youth.

4. Be aware of how the media portrays the "beautiful" people. An hour of MTV, a few teen magazines, and a stroll through a mall will give you insight on how our kids are being brainwashed.

5. Try to find an eating disorder specialist in your church or area and set up an appointment to discuss the topic with the person. This relationship, if

fruitful and comfortable, may serve as a referral for teenagers in your youth group who have eating disorders. Again, a program might develop from your visit.

To Help Teenagers With Eating Disorders:

1. Cut the fat jokes. Fun at the expense of our heavier youth group members erodes our ability to minister to them. And it is hardly honoring to Christ. The same goes if you hear a bulimic or anorexic joke. Walk what you talk! Practice what you preach! Would Jesus pull you aside with a, "Did you hear the one about the fat girl who..."?

2. Be honest and open in a loving, supportive way toward the kids you feel may have some eating disorder. Ask the hard questions if you notice strange eating habits, severe weight loss or gain, or other tip offs as discussed. Accept their answers, knowing that some will be denials and cover-ups. If their behavior in the future is incongruent with their statements, then meet with their parents. Literally, this may be a lifesaving action.

3. Be ready to offer alternatives when working with teenagers with eating disorders. Obese teenagers might not talk about their weight, but they may read about healthful eating and exercise. Your local hospital has a nutritionist on staff who can give you mountains of information about proper eating. Many popular women's magazines frequently publish good nutritional articles.

Obese teenagers often lack good information about what makes food good for you. Communicate sound information, not your personal biases. If you are a health food "nut" or a vegetarian, don't make your personal beliefs the gospel. Simply offer good, sound generalist advice.

For anorexic and bulimic teenagers, the tendencies are different. Skipping meals or overeating is common. So is the tendency to eat in response to anger, depression, anxiety, boredom, frustration, or loneliness. . .and then to purge. Again, nutritional information is important. But these kids need your love and to be supported as they work to develop a new body image. Remember, your support is more valuable when offered in conjunction with professional care and counseling.

4. Offering to accompany these teenagers to counseling appointments or group meetings is a wonderful support. Coordinate your participation with parents. Hurting people often love to talk about an intense problem. Chatting in the car can be a great time to reinforce what is being learned by the teenager.

5. If you are in a larger church with a number of people struggling with eating disorders, you might investigate starting a support group. Professionally trained leaders will be essential, but you can help to get the group on its feet and help in its ongoing needs.

And don't plan every activity around food!

To Help the Youth Group in General:
1. Don't ignore the problem. Add eating disorders to your vocabulary, especially when discussing that being a Christian does not make our problems disappear. I worked with one bulimic who confessed that, "I cried out to God and prayed the sinner's prayer over and over and over again with no change." She believed that becoming a Christian would eliminate her eating disorder.

Jesus does not promise that He will make everything perfect. He promises to be with us as we work through our problems.

2. A panel discussion concerning eating disorders must be handled sensitively. Those in the group who are hiding their anorexia or bulimia may panic if the topic is scheduled to be brought up. Those struggling with obesity, which cannot be hidden, will be embarrassed. Talk to the group beforehand, and with as many individuals as possible face-to-face. It will help to ease any tensions. This will work best if you've already built an atmosphere of trust and acceptance within the group.

Assemble a group of professionals who work with eating disorders, such as doctors, counselors, nutritionists, and psychologists, and with some who are in recovery from eating disorders. Don't be concerned if you can't find any "cured" folks. Most people in recovery programs see their recovery as a life-long process.

Let each panelist tell of their specific work or personal experience with eating disorders. Then, allow the kids to ask questions with your assistance. Often, professionally trained panel members will get bogged down by the jargon of their field. Ask them to clarify or interpret their comments. Don't assume that the kids understand what they are saying. Ask the questions which will bring out the answers that they need to hear.

3. Offer some studies which focus on how God sees us as His children. Jeremiah 29:11-13 tells us that God has, "...plans to prosper you and not to harm you, plans to give you hope and a future." That's great news to many of us. Jeremiah 31:3 guarantees us that He has, "loved us with an everlasting love." And Psalm 139:14 says, "I praise you because I am

fearfully and wonderfully made; your works are wonderful." That, too, is needed reassurance to many.

Be creative in your study and work to show that God's love is not based on the kinds of love we see in this media influenced society. Compare how the Bible guarantees God's acceptance and unconditional love to the kinds of messages we pick up from TV or magazines. If your skin isn't clear as glass, your waistline as slim as your wrist, and your clothes as stylish as the latest Paris fashion, the world says that you are of little value. Combat such thinking with the truth of God's Word.

12/ The Depressed Teenager

Julia's Story

Dad thinks that my "withdrawal times," as he calls them, are because I'm a teenager. Mom says she doesn't understand why I can't, "get my life together and be like the other kids." It hurts so much when they talk like this. I can't help it that I get depressed.

I've never talked about my depression before. What I know about depression I learned in health class and from reading about it at the library. My friend, Tia, says her parents make her go to a counselor for her bouts with depression. She says it helps and from what she's learned, I know I have depression.

One of the books said that depression is a condition where people have a lack of energy for living. That's me for sure. It's not that I'm mad or that my life is so complicated. It's not some stage of my development, either. It's more like a darkness that settles over me. My mind slows down, my body lacks any energy or strength, and I get angry with myself. I feel like I have a slow leak which drains the life out of me, and then I fill with gloom. Each day is a new burden. I feel hopeless and emotionally weak.

My older brother has been the only one willing to help me. He leaves me alone but takes time to tell me each day that he cares and that God cares. He's not pushy, but he says he's there to listen if I want to talk. That feels really good. . .but I never talk to him. What's the use? He keeps Mom and Dad off my back. They thought I was on drugs. He told them I'm not — which is the truth.

I guess that's all I want to say today. It feels good to talk, but I feel talked out. Maybe you could keep praying for me. I wish I knew how to stop it. I hate being depressed. . .God feels so far away.

When Darkness Is Within

Depression was once described to me as a "darkness that comes from within" by a young man who came to me for help. I assumed that he was being theological, talking about sin or evil. He told me that wasn't the kind of darkness he meant when he gets depressed. It was a darkness that inhibits his ability to see clearly the life that he was living. It's like the coming of night cloaking the countryside. There is no clarity, detail, or color. Only a gray heaviness that weighs on heart and mind.

For him it began when his parents divorced and his father moved to another state. His radically changing life triggered his depression. The changes were too much for him and he "shut down" inside for awhile.

Depression is characterized by feelings of sadness, listlessness, melancholia, the loss of pleasure to do almost anything, and the "blues." There may also be a reduction in mental activity and a lessening in physical activity. It is not uncommon for depressed people to complain of physical problems such as gastro-intestinal problems. Teenagers often complain of being extremely tired in the morning, even following a good night's sleep.

Other identifying signs of depression are:

—no longer looking forward to favorite activities
—increased irritability
—frequent complaints of headaches or stomach aches
—major changes in eating and sleeping patterns
—low energy, poor concentration, and a lasting boredom
—frequent absences from school, church, or other activities
—decline in participation and performance in activities
—changes in appetite
—excessive crying for no reason
—a new pessimism
—problems in decision making and memory.

Generally, if a teenager exhibits four of these symptoms over a two week period then professional help should be sought. However, before a counselor is sought, a general medical check-up is advised. A so-called "depressed" person may be experiencing diet, thyroid, or blood sugar changes that can only be resolved medically, not through counseling.

It's estimated that between 5 and 17 percent of all teenagers are depressed. For some, the depression is a long lasting, almost life-long problem of incredible persistence. Other teenagers find that the problem develops as a result of disturbances which change their lives. The divorce of parents, death of a close friend or grandparent, moving to another community, or school stress affect emotional balance.

Teenagers who seem to be miserable, unhappy, tearful, distressed, or possess low self-esteem are candidates for depression. This is especially true when that which used to be fun for them ceases to be. Talk of suicide or wishing that they had never been born are also good "red flags" for identifying depression.

If the darkness seems to be within, as with the young man above, you as the youth leader can offer relief through understanding and support. Society often fails to embrace depressed teenagers with compassion or acceptance. You'll be appreciated by these hurting young people for doing so.

Types of Depression

Depression is a catch-all for a number of problems. It is thought that over 10 million Americans suffer from various kinds of depressive disorders. Some believe as many as 5% of all adults struggle with depression. Add to this the families and friends who are also affected in their relationships and the picture becomes strikingly clear: Depression is a major source of pain for many families. Christians are not exempt.

Many who could benefit from treatment do not receive care because the disorder goes unrecognized. Misdiagnosis and inappropriate treatment is not unusual. With a success and recovery rate of about 80%, it is unfair for so many to remain deprived. As youth leaders, we can do much to help for our depressed teenagers.

There are numerous ways of defining depression. In the past 30 years this area has been researched heavily. For the youth worker a rudimentary level of knowledge is about all that is needed. We don't need to be psychologists or doctors to be helpful. Learning enough to recognize depression and then knowing what to do is powerful information.

Acute Depression is generally of short duration and characterized by boredom, less interaction with peers and friends, and social isolation. It is treatable and reversible. Onset may be sudden and it can be resolved without treatment as the "cloud of darkness" passes for the person. However, the experience may be very intense and troubling.

Chronic Depression is a more severe form and tends to have a more debilitating effect on teenagers. Being "world weary" and unable to perform normal, daily activities is not uncommon. Development is gradual and propelled by some type of negative experience that the teenager has had to face. Emotional trauma, constant rejection, or lasting, painful experiences would be examples.

Intensity levels of chronic depression seem to vary. Some report that the depressed mood remained with them for years. Teenagers with chronic depression have repeat episodes within five years of recovery in about 70% of the cases. This form of depression is difficult to treat even with medications and counseling.

Adolescents are also known to have *Masked Depression* which is difficult to recognize because the teenager covers the depression by acting out. These teenagers may attempt to cover their depression by being sexually promiscuous, going out often, or seeming to be active or involved in many social activities. The attempt is to cover the depression and to deny its existence by high, almost manic, activity. Feeling lonely, abandoned, and generally depressed, these teenagers may use drugs and alcohol, juvenile delinquency, and other negative avenues in an attempt to escape the depression. They may seem to be restless and angry. Key here is the effort to mask the depression by other behaviors that throw the observer off the trail of the heart of the matter.

Other types of depression may be linked with psychological disturbances such as bipolar depression, secondary depression, and manic-depression. These should be treated by professionals.

Many of our not-quite-adult young people experience depression as a reaction to other things which make her or him feel out of control and helpless. This fosters self-doubt and may lead to a generally depressed attitude. Major losses, such as divorce, death, moving, a church split, a pastor leaving, serious illness, and others can start the depression. Losses which we, as adults, might underestimate, could include a break up with a close friend, the loss of virginity, the onset of sexual activity in males and females alike, flunking a test or class, missing an important school or church function, or the like. Don't judge their reaction! How they feel is the most significant clue to the depth of their pain. It is to this pain that we are called as we work to "bind up the brokenhearted" (Isaiah 61:1).

Depression and Christianity

For millions of Christians who occasionally experience depression, the church may not be the most sympathetic place to find help. Sermons often mandate that we "live in victory," "be joyful," and "overcome all things." Christians who are depressed may feel that the church is an adversary. Yet, Scripture portrays the truth of a God who wants all people to walk confidently in His love and acceptance.

Numerous biblical characters served God yet suffered bouts of depression. Elijah became so depressed following his victories that he wanted to die. Jonah became depressed when God would not do as he requested and, under the gourd, he told God that he regretted his birth. The same occurred with Job who, following great losses in his personal life, became depressed. God's witness to each of us who deal with depression is that He stood with these Bible figures in their pain. And He will do so for us!

As youth workers, we can communicate that depression is normal as a reaction to life's stress. If we constantly preach to our teenagers that "victory is in Jesus" without reminding them that Jesus also came to heal the hurting and love the sinner, we do them a disservice. We do have victory in Christ, but not at every turn and certainly not always immediately. That is how God allows us to learn lessons on how to grow closer to Him. God's people can learn to recognize and face depression with the assurance that God, the church, and loved ones will be there to assist and support. This position is a more helpful and a wiser approach when ministering to depressed young people.

Coping With Depression

To help depressed teenagers find relief, I repeat that encouraging a medical examination is a wise first step if the depression has lasted between two weeks and a month. A doctor can determine if the depression is caused by a physical condition.

If it's not medical, work with the teenager to see if she or he will open up and talk about feelings. Has something happened? What has changed? Probe gently and quit if resistance is experienced. Let the teenager know that you are available to talk. Depression is a normal part of life, that includes Christians.

For prolonged depression, offer your youth a valuable service by giving support, understanding, and a listening ear. Be accepting. Provide literature which can be read. Remember that these teenagers lack the energy for normal living. Simply giving someone a booklet on depression will not insure that it will be read. Read it with them.

Some information which teenagers find helpful:

• Depression usually lasts only a few days and is a normal part of the give and take of life.

• Rest, as in the story of Elijah, often provides immediate relief.

• Sharing the story of why one is depressed is often miraculous in relieving it.

• Doing something fun, even if you don't feel like it, can make you feel better.

• Working on a positive approach to life is invaluable in keeping one's spirits up; it helps one to feel better.

• Repeatedly take the problem and the depression to the Lord "because He cares for you" (I Peter 5:7).

Being with people who care, knowing that friends are praying, and having the chance to talk about it all help the depressed teenager to understand the hurt and relieve the pain.

As youth leaders we do well to accept that this is one of the largest difficulties among today's youth. Making ourselves available to them when they face depression works miracles. Be careful not to confuse depression with disinterest. Be accepting of those in your group who struggle with this problem and have no energy for life.

Programming Ideas

For You:

1. Read, read, read. Research provides us with

new information almost daily. It is in your best interest to remain current on depression. Since depression is so common to all humans, the newspapers, news magazines, TV talk shows, and other media sources cover it regularly. There are numerous Christian books on depression which are helpful, too.

2. Reflect upon your own times of depression. Most of us have struggled with occasional depression and have some insights if we'll pause and examine our lives. What has worked for you? Who reached out and helped? What frustrated you? How did you bring new light to illuminate your darkness? Take some time and evaluate how depression interfered with your life and relationships. Use this personal information to guide your understanding of depressed teenagers in your youth group.

3. Keep a supply of informational literature on hand for personal use and to hand out to the teenagers. Write the following sources for information. There may be a minor charge for some of the materials. Some are free.

•National Mental Health Assoc., 1021 Prince St., Alexandria, Virginia, 22314-2971.

•National Alliance For The Mentally Ill, 2101 Wilson Boulevard, Suite 302, Arlington, Virginia, 22201.

•National Foundation for Depressive Illness, 20 Charles St., New York, NY, 10014.

•National Depressive and Manic Depressive Assoc., 53 West Jackson Boulevard, Room 618, Chicago, Ill., 60604.

For the Depressed Teenager:

1. Offer to accompany depressed teenagers to see a Christian counselor. Referrals become important if

the depression becomes long-lasting. We must accept that this is one area out of our expertise. Yet, that doesn't need to stop us from being supportive. Many teenagers will appreciate having you chauffeur them to the office and wait for them. Of course, such help must be coordinated with the parents. Many parents will recognize your important and unique role in the lives of their teenagers. Being there for the teenager and the family is good ministry and reminds each family member of the abiding Christ.

2. Consider offering a support group for depressed teens. It is a great help to them to hear of others' experiences with depression. The format could be simply talking it over with a time for prayer. Group projects could be assigned to research depression. Bi-weekly groups work well.

A colleague who suffered from depression for most of her life found out about a new treatment medication through such a group. She talked to her doctor and now she lives without the major, debilitating effects of depression. Today she is working as a Christian Education Supervisor.

3. The Psalms are one of the best sources of spiritual aid for depressed teenagers. So many Psalms reflect David's struggles with his understanding of life, justice, his relationship with God and others, and his disappointments. While his confessions begin with depressing words of how he sees things, they always conclude with some beautiful statement which puts it all into perspective.

While literally dozens of Psalms minister to the depressed heart and mind, Psalms 27, 28, and 103 are especially good. When talking of God's loving attributes and marvelous power, many find the "blues" changing to a rosier hue.

4. Encouragement is a wonderful tool in working with hurting kids. Even if a depressed teenager is in counseling, you can still be their "listening ear." Be a major source of support, but don't usurp the professional work of the counselor or doctor.

Many teenagers need us to be a sounding board. Referring them does not mean we are finished with them. Let them know that.

For the Youth Group:

1. Professionals in our communities offer many sources for helping depressed teenagers. We can facilitate the sharing of this information. Not only can the church offer depressed teenagers help, but so can physicians, psychologists, social workers, community mental health centers, university medical and psychological centers, family service agencies, counseling centers, and the like. Letting the whole group know that help is easily found and there is no shame in seeking it is a wonderful gift.

2. Invite a panel of the above professionals in for a full and open discussion of depression. Begin the meeting with prayer and the reading of one of David's Psalms that express so well his times of depression. State that even Bible characters became bogged down by depression, so it should not surprise us when we, too, become depressed.

Let the professionals cover the kinds of depression, the treatment options, and related topics. Question the panel about how common depression is on our society. Personal struggles with depression really hit home when shared.

3. Hold a similar meeting as above for the parents of your youth group. Educating parents will go a long way in helping kids deal with depression.

4. Plan a "Depression Experience." Sitting in small groups (with each one led by an adult advisor), ask the kids to talk about the state of the world, school, church, their love life, politics, pollution, racism, sin, death — anything that isn't going right. You'll find the small groups creating for themselves a mood of depression.

When this mood has affected every group, bring the kids together and talk about how it would feel to live in this mood for weeks, or months, at a time. Assure them that some people do. This helps the kids to understand that depression is a very real experience that millions face daily.

Show them that hope is available by breaking the mood. Lead them in talking themselves out of the depression. You can do this by "counting blessings" or talking about positive, wholesome, constructive things. Close with prayer by thanking God for being there for us in every mental, emotional, physical, and spiritual need. Finally, show a cartoon video to make sure the heaviness is really broken.

5. Involve the kids in some character studies of servants of God who experienced depression. Again, David, Elijah, Job, and Jonah make excellent studies. Show them that what made the difference with these people was their relationship with God. In the midst of their pain, they called out to God for help. Develop from these stories some solid ideas for combating depression. Talk about what it would be like to be called to do God's work and deal with depression. Assure the teenagers that many in your church and youth group face exactly that.

Being depressed and being a Christian are not inconsistent with each other. Christians do encounter depression, as much as anyone. Yet, in Jesus Christ we have the promise of His presence and care. Sharing this with your teenagers goes a long way to producing healthy, fruitful Christian young people.

13/ The "Nerdy" Teenager

Stuart's Story

I don't fully understand what the differences are. I know I'm not like other kids. But everyone seems to think that "my kind" are all alike and should get together at Chess Club or Physics Club to "relate." Yet, even when I'm with the other "misfits," I feel as though the group isn't for me. Actually, I feel like I have no group. There is no place for me.

Mom seems to hate me for being different. She says she loves me, but then she says, "Why can't you be like the other kids?" I'd like to fit in. I just don't. I know that I embarrass her and Dad. I'm always apologizing for being me.

School is so easy that I feel robbed. I dream of the challenges of college. Nothing stumps me for very long. When I get the gist of the problem, the solution comes with almost no effort. I understand that I am gifted, but I wish I were like the other kids.

I'm a loner at school. But not by choice. It's survival because the other kids hurt me rather than befriend me. They reject me for who I am. In truth, I'm really not a loner. . .just lonely.

Some classes are better than others. My art teacher likes me because my work is so "fresh" and "original." My music theory teacher says I have advanced tastes. Both are trying to help me and be my friend, but having teacher friends is somehow unnatural. It certainly doesn't endear me to the other kids. I want friends my own age.

I believe that God loves me, but I have to wonder why He made me this smart. Being intelligent shouldn't be a handicap. But I feel like I'm cursed.

I'll have to wait and see if the youth group will accept me. I like the kids and the games and all of the surface acceptance. I'm waiting for the letdown. The whisper of "nerd" or "weirdo" will come in time. It always does. Someone will call me "Mr. Mega-Brains" or tease me because I ask questions. I hate being made fun of that way. Until that happens, I'll keep coming. I really feel like you're trying to understand me and accept me.

Some people just never quite fit in. They're always an outsider. That's me. Bright, but harmless...and unwanted.

I believe it when you tell me about God's love and how the church is home to all who love and accept Christ. That's real inviting. But the other kids don't seem to know it. It's hard to be trusting and accepting when you're different. But your kindness helps.

Through the Cracks

There are no statistics on "nerdy" kids. No special studies or reports. Yet, we all have them in some form in our groups. It's easy to let them slip through the cracks.

Usually, in the junior and early senior high years, the Nerdy teenager remains a regular in youth group. Then, many of them drop out of youth group with a mumbled excuse like, "School's demanding a lot from me." In reality, the pain has become unbearable. They received the message that youth group, like so much of their world, wouldn't accept them.

Nerdy teenagers are regular kids with a different approach or outlook of life. They are smart, often brilliant. They may be precocious in art, literature, music, or almost any academic subject. They may dress differently. Some seem to have no fashion sense while others dress in a strange, alternative manner. Some are simply bizarre in their garb.

They ask questions which some of us wonder about but few can answer. They may think differently and perceive life in a different light. Understanding them can be difficult because they are, in reality, more intelligent than many of us. They often are expert in some area.

Nerds don't set out to be different. It is their essential self. They are not weird, or attention seekers, or "brains" in that they have more intelligence than the rest of us. They are set apart by virtue of their superior intellect or talents. Remember, a key to the adolescent years is conformity. For many teenagers, a 4.0 average is hard work. For Nerds it may be a cinch.

Nerds do not try to be abnormal. They do not avoid the normal teenage culture. It is merely not who they are. And there is nothing more sad than a Nerd who tries to act like all the other kids.

These intelligent young people love God! They communicate with God through prayer like the rest of us. They grow in the Lord and can minister powerfully through Christ. They need the church and the church needs them. Yet, so often churches don't quite know where to use the more artistic types and may inadvertently reject their contributions and feelings.

My friend, James, would fit the Nerd category. He is artistically and musically creative and well read in classical literature. He dresses very differently and sees life, and matters of faith, through different eyes. He is spontaneous, dramatic, and wonderful. However, he has felt discriminated against by Christians because he could not fit into a mold. Well meaning believers have ridiculed his hairstyles, his art work, his tastes in music and his interest in literature. Because of this rejection, Jaymes left the church community he so dearly loved. To his credit he did not leave his Lord and sought fellowship elsewhere.

Nerds are often taken more seriously in college, if they choose to attend. They are challenged. Their divergent ideas are considered more seriously by other students and professors. They find a climate of acceptance for their non-normative approach to life and the world. While this is refreshing to them, it is often tragic for the church.

All too often Nerds discover that the church has no place for them. I know many who are antagonistic to church life and the Christian faith. If asked why, they often respond with a heartbreaking story of how fellow believers hurt or crushed them or their God-given talents. As youth leaders, we must be sensitive and not allow this unintentional rejection to continue.

Life as a Nerd - Some Observations

I am not aware of anything written on Nerds. However, we can identify some characteristics which help us to recognize their special needs. In general they:

—tend to be somewhat smarter than other kids.

—tend not to fit into the larger group but may excel in small group or individual activities.

—may see life in a somewhat different light when compared to the perceptions of most other youth.

—seem to be drawn to the offbeat, the strange, the unconventional, the bizarre or the unorthodox.

—seem to get the message by senior high school that they are better off as a "loner."

—ask unanswerable questions, but not in mockery or to stump you. They really think about these things.

—may come to meetings late and leave early to avoid painful or uncomfortable interaction with other youth.

—often may appear introverted. However, I have found that this is often not the real person; it is a protective barrier.

—are typically referred to by the other kids as a nerd, weirdo, brain, bookworm or other distinguishing label which indicates high intellectual ability...and some degree of mockery.

—often possess a dry, insightful wit that is frequently respected and enjoyed by other kids. For many Nerds this witty humor is the only point of ingress into the group.

—can seem to be unhealthy in appearance and are often non-athletic. They may hate sports or games which seem to be tedious and nonsensical.

—seem to be aloof and preoccupied.

—may appear to be ignoring lessons or announcements, only to be able to repeat it completely if asked.

—tend to project an air of superiority as a defense.

—are involved or interested in politics, social issues, environmental concerns, and world affairs well beyond the normal level for those their age.

—are passionate and idealistic.

—are typically very knowledgeable about any subject that interests them.

It is obvious that many teenagers fit some of these descriptions. It is when most of these descriptions apply that the teenager is a Nerd by the definition of her or his own peers.

Nerds are gifted in a variety of ways and have the potential to be valuable contributors to the youth programs of your church. But they are a group with special needs, concerns, and ministry challenges. As leaders we must be sensitive if we intend to make the youth group a relevant place in their lives. Every teenager is unique and special.

I wonder how the Apostle Paul would have fared in our youth groups. He was a Nerd. He describes himself as being at the head of his class. He followed all of the rules and did exactly what he was supposed to do. He was the perfect student and refers to himself as "faultless" (Philippians 3:4-6).

We would not overlook the needs of a Paul. We should feel the same about our other "less cool" teenagers.

One word of caution concerning your attitude toward Nerds. Treat them as regular teenagers, for they are. It is their peer culture that labels them and separates them. Don't participate in this alienation as their youth worker. Accept, love, nurture, value, and include them.

Finally, there is some truth in the saying, "Nerds grow up and rule the world." I have received much back, both personally and professionally, from the Nerds that I took the time to invest in. They grew out of the Nerd stage into marvelous women and men. As teenagers they didn't quite fit in. As adults, they have become wonderful ministry partners and many are active in our church. In giving them a home in the church when they were in need of a "place," we found our bread coming back upon the waters in their devotion to the Lord as adults.

Programming Ideas

Nerds are not as specialized as other groups of kids. They represent a wide variety of teenagers. As a result, programming approaches need to consider the breadth of their varied experiences. Don't fall into the trap of trying to make something "fit" when it is wrong in approach. Such insensitivity further strengthens their case against society, church included. Initially, be yourself and simply love and accept them.

For You:

1. Talk to the Nerds in your group individually. They may seem similar on the outside, but they will be very different teenager to teenager. Find out how they feel about themselves. How do they define themselves? What do they think about their world? Their school? Their family or church or peers? I have found that most will welcome the chance to talk. For many the hurt runs deep. They are different, not deviant.

2. Find out how they feel about church and the youth group. Do they see themselves as part of the group? Or are they just hanging out because they are lonely and the youth group is less painful?

You may be surprised to discover that any given Nerd will not perceive her or himself as being similar to other Nerds in the group. Nerds tend to see themselves as completely different from other Nerds.

For the Nerdy Teenager:

1. Like other kids, these kids are in the group for basic, normal human needs of affiliation with others. Snag them by promoting genuine group acceptance with allowances for difference. This begins with you. If you hesitate in your love, acceptance, and understanding, the rest of the group will follow your lead. If leadership reinforces acceptance, the rest of the group will be less destructive. Never single them out with comments like, "Jane always has an answer," or "Tom's a brain; he'll know."

2. Some of my youth work colleagues have had a difficult time in accepting the notions and thinking of Nerds. Yet, often Nerds don't care as much about being accepted as they do about being heard. They experience constant rejection in their world.

You can give them the gift of honest and active listening, even if you don't understand their wavelength. Let them have an appropriate forum for discussion and comment, but be balanced. A number of youth Bible studies have been literally destroyed by allowing too much debate and discussion. Too much time was given to ideas and not enough to God's Word.

I find that Nerds respect honest "give and take" in discussion. They are more interested in the flow of ideas and the chance to be a part of the group than in being "right" or having the last word. "I don't know" doesn't seem to bother them, either.

3. When guided, Nerds make wonderful leaders and helpers in youth group. If accepted by their peer group, they will stick with the group through any

ups and downs. As with any teenager, you must be willing to disciple them.

Naturally, your first reaction is, "Certainly I'll disciple them!" Yet, it may be different discipling a Nerd. Especially if you tend to be very gregarious and un-nerdish. These kids are going to seem bizarre or ridiculous at times. But the investment is worth it.

Once I worked with two sisters in a senior high youth group setting who were nerdish. I spent a good deal of time with them and made a conscious effort to include these two. I gave credence to their "off-the wall" questions and comments. I learned to enjoy their strange humor and different thinking. In time, they became the closest thing to teenage Bible scholars I have ever seen. Later, when I needed some help, one of them stepped forward and began working with the junior high youth group. When I took another pastorate, they continued to aid the youth programs and helped to maintain a post-high school program in the church.

Other Nerds have counseled at church camp for me with great sensitivity and love. A number have gone into various forms of Christian ministry. They received love and acceptance when they needed it. Now they are an asset to God's work.

4. At times you will find a Nerd in need of counseling. For some, the whole concept of counseling is difficult. They are so rationally-based that they can be destitute in terms of understanding their feelings. Some seem to have no sense of inner person. They prefer the scientific method as an answer to all of life's problems.

When counseling is offered, it is not unusual to find it a terribly unsatisfying experience for the Nerd. Feelings may be foreign and closed off. Emotions may be deeply buried. It takes gentle encouragement to connect them with their feelings. Having been hurt by peers, many have learned not to feel. This can also be evident in cases where parents have little insight into their kid's uniqueness. Being there for them and letting them talk is amazingly liberating for them.

For the Youth Group:

1. Teach the kids to appreciate the variety within the body of Christ. First Corinthians is a marvelous exercise in understanding diversity. Lead the group in celebrating any special-life situation. Show them that there is nothing wrong with Nerds or Jocks or Barbies or any other small group which has some identity within the larger group. These roles reflect value systems and personal, particular identities. It is who they see themselves as being. These identities give them a hand-hold on daily living by helping them to define life. Present the biblical glory of the wonders of variety in the people God surrounds us with.

2. If a particular Nerd in the group is willing, you might let him or her describe what it is like being seen as a Nerd. In their testimony they can do much to break down how teenagers treat others. This has proven to be a successful way to help the group treat the individual differently. Most kids don't want to be mean and heartless. They fall into ruts of expected behavior and thoughtlessly continue acting that way. Or they follow a crowd mentality.

Don't undertake such an exercise without preparation. It is unfair to simply tell the teenager to "go for it." Discuss beforehand their testimony and what they wish to communicate with the youth group. Prepare her or him about the responses they may receive. It is not uncommon for those more verbal to see the evening as an opportunity to "roast" someone. Use an older, more secure teenager.

No other teenager requires you to be more intuitive than the Nerds. The balancing act you must perform is significant. You will need to give space while also making efforts to be inclusive. Other types of teenagers have been fully researched while the Nerds have not. They have always been with us, but never considered in terms of needs and ministry opportunities. They are easily overlooked since their special-life situation is not characterized by some disorder or dysfunction. Sensitivity is the key word. When reached for Christ, these teenagers respond in healthy, effective ways that touch others.

14/ Low Income Teenagers

Jenny's Story

My name is Jenny and I attend Grace Church. I love the pastor and the youth group is the greatest. But I don't go much anymore.

Since Dad's plant closed last summer, we've been pretty broke. Mom still works part time and Dad gets unemployment, but we have to watch every penny. I don't mind too much. I feel bad for my sister because she's too young to understand why we don't go to play miniature golf or out to eat anymore. We manage, though, and Dad says he has some good leads for work. Mom keeps reminding us that God has been very good to us, and we still have our home and food. It's just one of those things. I'm not too upset, except with my youth group.

I never realized how expensive it was to be a "good" Christian until Dad lost his job. Before, I assumed that the kids not going on retreats and trips were not interested in our group. I never missed a meeting or activity. I didn't have to miss because we could afford it. Now that I can't afford to attend the activities, I have to wonder how many others are being excluded from youth group simply because they're poor?

Poor. That's a dirty word in our culture. I've discovered that we treat the poor or those with low incomes exactly how the label implies — lower class. That may be my new label. . .but I know that God still sees me as first class!

I guess I can't blame the youth leaders. I shouldn't expect them to custom make the group to fit my needs. I wish I could tell them that I can't afford to attend. They've visited me to see why I've missed so many meetings, but. . . .You'd think they'd know. Everyone knows my dad's out of work.

I'm sure things will be back to normal when Dad gets one of those jobs. Until then, I'll just try to endure the anger and confusion I feel inside. But now my thinking has changed. Now I know why some of the other kids don't attend. I wish I knew what to do.

Getting to Know the Low Income Teenager

Jenny's story is like so many in our youth groups. She is poor, proud, and uncertain how to handle this special-life situation. She has found that the youth program at church is too expensive for her family's current financial picture. She has discovered the difficulty of being in a low income family, even if only temporarily. Additionally, she is too embarrassed to communicate the problem to her youth leaders — youth leaders who know that her dad has lost his job but haven't made the connection.

The effects of poverty or low income upon our teenagers are very observable. The guys often display an "attitude" of indifference. They may compensate for being poor by lying or exaggeration. Some seem to feel they have "something to prove" and, in fact, they do. They want the rest of the group to see them as valuable. And sadly, many young people become "snobs" when a poorer teen enters the group, adding to the teenager's pain.

Girls are likely to be less aggressive than guys. Some try to be invisible and avoid attention-getting situations while others may engage in over compensation as a means of equalizing the obvious inequalities. Like Jenny, they feel embarrassed and are not willing to let others know how tough things really are.

A tip off to poverty is that low income kids are generally less anxious to have you, as youth leader, visit them at home. Check out your suspicions by locating their street addresses. If the neighborhood is unknown to you, do a secret drive through. Is it a poor section of town? If so, this is probably the source of their resistance. If the section is not generally poorer, the tip off may be recent unemployment or another problem such as abuse or family discord.

Other characteristics which help to identify low income teenagers are a sense of hopelessness, powerlessness or despair, and some have trouble gaining specialized skills or knowledge. These "defeatist attitudes" are seen typically with kids who have lived within a culture of poverty for all or most of their lives.

Some tip-offs for recognizing teenagers of families who are experiencing some kind of reduction in available money may include:

—The family structure changes through divorce, death, remarriage, etc.

—They suddenly drop out of the church, youth group, school activities, and other social functions which require money for participation.

—A plant in your area closes.

—A general decline in appearance, attitude, or other changes in self-care.

Some of these changes may be due to other adolescent conflicts (drugs, abuse, etc.) or regular teenage development. But any sudden changes in a teenager are good reasons for a closer look.

Some Shocking Figures

Currently, the poverty level in the United States is the average standard for the rest of the world. Most humans do not enjoy luxuries. For some, simple necessities like shelter, clothing, and food are absent. Yet, the poor survive and function remarkably well when all is considered. And while Jesus said the poor would be with us always (Deuteronomy 15:11; Matthew 26:11), as Christians we must never accept poverty as the standard. Jesus challenges us to action (Matthew 25:31-46; James 2:14-24).

The United States is blessed with the highest standard of living in the world. Our poor are not as poor as those in other parts of the world. This makes it all too easy for us to overlook the needs of the poor in our country. Often we hide them away in neighborhoods invisible to most of us. However, our poor still starve to death, still die from the cold, and live in a moment to moment existence.

A new phenomena is being found in our nation's better neighborhoods. Here, in lovely suburbia, an estimated 15.6 million persons, referred to as "displaced families," struggle for their daily needs. They live in nice houses, even fancy at times, and inside they live in poverty. Displaced homemakers are most often women who have experienced a change in income due to divorce, separation, or widowhood. Other displaced families may be in this difficult position through long-term unemployment, medical problems, or disability. This unusual population of poverty-level families rose 12% between 1980 and 1990.

Visiting these families can be shocking. A beautiful, landscaped home may be almost empty of furnishings. Yet, these families hang on to the facade of success in hopes that it will return to them.

Add to this unexpected group the traditionally poor and our figures skyrocket. Consider these statistics on the poor in the United States:

- There are an estimated 35.5 million Americans who are considered to be poor.
- Of these, over 13 million are children.
- One in four children live on welfare at some point in life.
- Poverty levels are falling in rural areas but increasing in metropolitan areas. In 1987, there were 23.4 million US residents living in metro areas classified as poor.
- While the traditional, stereotypical explanation for poverty is laziness, it is increasingly obvious that the true sources are such dynamics as recession, unemployment, low wages, inadequate job skills, and the lack of available jobs.
- One out of four children under the age of six lives in poverty. Forty percent of the children in young families are poor.
- The poverty rate increased to 11.5% in 1991.
- Nearly one-half of all black children and one-sixth of all white children live in poverty.
- Over 11 million Americans make wages lower than $4.00 per hour. This wage is not enough to lift a family of three above the poverty level.

Low income can result from some unexpected situation like unemployment, divorce, death, family crisis, serious illness, money management problems, or salary reduction. It can also be the result of a family's inability to produce a livable income. Factors like education, mental and physical health, the financial climate of a particular area in an economic depression, and the wage earning abilities of parents may all prevent an increase in family income.

Finally, a family may be low income due to alcoholism or drug addiction, gambling, refusal to work, a habitual welfare mentality, or other such problems.

Our Christian commitment is to every person. To share the gospel means we must include these "invisible" people, whom we may not see — or choose not to recognize. Christ had some radical things to say about the relationship of money, spirituality, and other people. To minister to poorer families, families often missed in our churches and youth groups, we need to first come to terms with Jesus' teachings about poverty.

Jesus and Money Issues

My favorite accounts about Jesus and such subjects as the poor, wealth, money, and poverty come from the Bible's own "money man," Matthew the tax collector. Related subject studies on topics such as poverty, rich, and riches will yield insights into Christ's expectations of us.

Jesus valued people, never possessions. In His conversation with the rich young man in Matthew 19:16-30, Jesus suggests that he sell his possessions and "give to the poor." The man sadly turns away because, "he had great wealth."

I wonder how often the material world has blocked our blessings from the Lord? Jesus points out that faith is difficult for the rich. His conclusion in verse 30, "But many who are first will be last, and many who are last will be first" is more than a joke for those at the end of the potluck line. In our society, the poor are definitely in a last place position.

Other verses worthy of note include:

• Matthew 6:24, Jesus proclaims we cannot serve "both God and money."

• Matthew 13:22, He reminds us that the "deceitfulness of wealth" is part of what chokes our spiritual life.

• Matthew 10:1-10, a biblical philosophy of money, material possessions, and ministry.

• Matthew 26:11, Jesus reminds us that the poor are with us and need our care and ministry. Too often we use this as an excuse to overlook them.

• Matthew 11:5 says much of what convicts me concerning ministry to the poor. This account focuses on the kinds of miracles John the Baptist's disciples were instructed to relate to John as proof of Christ's fulfillment as the Messiah. Jesus concludes with, ". . .and the good news is preached to the poor." This is as much a sign of God's presence as the most dramatic miracle.

General Recommendations

Jenny is in crisis. Her youth leaders, other youth group members, and her church may all be adding to the crisis by not reaching out to all the "Jennys" in their town or group. Unintentionally, all sides are operating in denial. Denial is the most comfortable, but least effective, means by which a crisis may be managed. We seem to feel that if we act like it isn't there, it will go away.

Jenny needs her church. . .and her church needs her. Jesus instructed us not to exclude those with low incomes. His directives included clothing and feeding and making room for them in our hearts, lives, and churches. Matthew 25:31-46 graphically depicts how important it is to minister to the poor. In doing so we minister to Jesus Himself.

Money should not be a factor which excludes others from the body of Christ. However, if we are not actively sensitive to this special-life situation, those without means may slip through our fingers...and out of our hearts.

Perhaps a good way to regain and keep those within your youth programs who may be in financial difficulties is to rethink your entire program from the position of "no dough." Look at your activities from the last six months. What did it cost to come to each activity? What was the total cost for the six months? Did the church subsidize any of the amount? Were fund-raisers used to offset costs?

List the kids in your group who have dropped out over the last year. Why did they drop out? Was it a matter of trying the group and not liking it? Or might there be a financial reason?

Do a finance check on your church. If you change your program and target new, poorer teenagers, economically hard hit churches can experience prosperity — not of money, but of precious young people.

In some cases, this factor of families struggling with low incomes can explain the majority of the difficulties in a youth program. Northeast Ohio saw incredible industrial growth in the '50s and '60s. Major industries like automobiles, steel, and rubber built huge empires in Akron, Cleveland, and Youngstown. Life was good and churches flourished ...until the '70s when these companies closed their doors and moved to the south.

There is no reason why youth work successes need to be weighed by how expensive a program is. Yet, good is often equated with a large budget, big name speakers and performers being "rented," and many kinds of activities. Frankly, in some of the churches I've visited, I couldn't afford to be the Youth Pastor on the amount I earn on a pastor's salary!

Programming Ideas

For You:

1. Become aware of the true economic picture of your community. From what sections of the community do you draw your youth group participants? Are the kids predominately poor? Or better off? We are called to minister to our communities in Christ's name. If we are excluding poorer families in that community, we are missing our call.

2. Discover what social services are available for the teenagers in your group. State and county welfare or social service offices sponsor great programs to encourage poor teenagers through job training, tutoring, college money, and job application help, to name a few. Knowing about these services will make you truly helpful to your teenagers who need these services.

3. Spend some time in self-reflection about your personal attitudes on poverty and poor people. What was your experience growing up? Did you dine well and shop at the better stores? Or did you shop at second-hand stores and rarely eat out? Our past influences and colors our present.

If you were poor, you may have to wrestle with bitterness or bad attitudes toward those who do have more. Check those attitudes to make sure that they serve God.

All of us have blind spots, areas in which we cannot see our true selves. Attitudes toward the poor are common grounds for un-Christlike points of view. Talk to someone you trust about the possibility of having unhealthy blind spots toward the poor. You may not be able to see them, but others certainly will.

To Help Low Income Teenagers:

1. Create a job center. I often get calls for teenagers to help with lawn work, clean up, chores, babysitting, pet sitting, and the like. These are genuine services for people in need who feel genuinely appreciative when someone can be found to help out. A job board with opportunities for youth employment can be easily developed. Posted opportunities make jobs available to everyone and remove any shame.

2. Start a small company. You or some other willing adult with skills in an area could form a summer company to help the kids who don't have jobs. As a former carpenter, I have accepted jobs like roofing, painting, minor remodeling, landscaping, and repairs. I would line up work for the kids committed to the program, take them with me to estimate the jobs, gather the materials, and then train them to do the tasks. We would advertise in the church bulletin and monthly newsletter. At times, we called the local newspaper's "Around Town" column for free publicity.

This effort takes a lot of time, energy, and will amount to hard work. The reward is that you and your low income teenagers can accomplish some great things together, often benefiting church members who need work done but simply cannot pay a professional. It is a dual mission — the kids and those needing the services. Often our services were requested by elderly persons or single parents who lived on fixed incomes. We were the answer to their prayers, as they were to ours.

3. Lead low income kids through the job hunting process. An excellent way to break the poverty mentality, which believes, "I'm poor now and will be forever so why try at all," is to educate teenagers about job hunting, resumes, and skill development.

An excellent resource is *What Color Is Your Parachute?* by Richard Nelson Bolles. In this book you will have literally all you need to educate the kids about the job market.

For the Entire Group:
1. Work to equalize the involvement of low income teenagers and group members from higher income families. One way is to compile a list of the free activities in your area. Include all of the parks as well as available activities each one offers. Programming ideas can be developed around these free places that will be memorable.

For example, take the kids to an airport. The hugeness of the jets, the excitement of the travelers, the hustle and bustle is electrifying.

You can explore the airport for a while and then sit down and tell made up stories about the travelers. Ask the kids about particular travelers. Where do you think she came from? Where is he going? Is that man running from something? If you were on the plane next to that person, what would you tell them about yourself? Your life? Your faith? Some airports may give you a tour of the inner facilities.

Talk about fantasy travels. If you could travel anywhere, where would you go? This kind of play is not only free and fun, it also helps the teenagers imagine themselves in a different light. It expands their world and helps supply them with dreams. Don't forget to take a world atlas. Most U.S. teenagers test poorly in world geography.

Other free events to add to your list would be museums, art galleries, university programs, other area church programs, school events, and community activities. Watch the newspaper in the "This Week" section for new and novel offerings. Work from your list as you program the youth group's activities' calendar.

2. Make up a list of the "cheap" activities available in your area. Some museums and art galleries have a small admission price. Sporting events often offer an inexpensive, general admission or group rates. Volleyball in the park, tennis for everyone, a baseball game on a local diamond, a hike, or a day fishing are great activities. Also, the zoo is always a hit! There's a lot to be said for those things in life that are inexpensive. Also, you help give the kids ideas about inexpensive dates for their own social times together.

3. When planning a major activity, plan far enough ahead to insure that low income kids will be able to save or adequately fund-raise so they can participate.

When my teenagers wanted to go from Ohio to Florida for a major youth rally, we began working toward the goal six months in advance. We raised $5,000.00 in those six months. Everyone who wanted to go attended. Not bad, considering many of the kids were from welfare or low income families. Most of the teenagers had never been out of our state or seen the ocean.

4. Make sure the kids raise money *together* for a single, big event. Whether a trip, retreat, or church

camp, it is important for the kids to be lumped together in fund-raising — low income and higher income alike. Sometimes a well-to-do teenager will want to bow out of the group fund-raising activities and just pay the full price of registration up front. Unless there is a good reason, like a job or a sports schedule that requires a high commitment, take the position that each teenager has to help earn the registration costs. This will equalize the group and keep them working together.

5. Enlist your congregation in some type of campership, scholarship, or sponsorship program.

For over 35 years my home church has been committed to paying half of the registration fee for any young person who wishes to go to church camp. This is extended to the richest and the poorest kids in the church. The church is not rich; it is just committed to church camping.

This commitment has been costly. In 1968, when only 8 attended, the campership cost per teenager was $17.00. In 1990, 32 kids went to camp and the camperships cost $75.00 each. Of the 32 who went in 1990, only 7 could have actually paid the full price of camp. Programs which aid all of the church's teenagers don't put the low income kids in any kind of charity category.

6. The kids who cannot pay the other half of a sponsored activity need to be given a chance to work. This is as much a part of helping kids grow in Christ as the most spiritual tidbit you might share at Bible study. Let's face it, it is often easier to do the work ourselves, as adults, than it is to invite a carload of kids in to do it for us.

But find jobs for the kids to do. We lined up jobs from those who had work that needed to be done. The "wages" are donations from the person receiving the work or service and are not revealed to the kids. They may give whatever they can for the job.

One year, to earn money for a special trip, the low income kids washed a house trailer for a donation of $5.00 and then cleaned out a small pond for a donation of $250.00. Each task was done with diligence and zeal. I coordinated the tasks, transported the kids, planned the work, lined up the tools, and distributed the money among the kids. That's what it takes to make sure that low income teenagers are part of our ministries.

7. Let the "rich" help the "poor." Compile a list of folks in the church who have a genuine spirit of giving. These people will often give to insure a teenager from a low income family has a chance to participate. But they won't want to give arbitrarily. Bring the needs to their attention and ask them to pray about helping. If they are able, they will come through for the kids. It's a good idea to have the kids send a thank you note, through you, to their anonymous donor.

This list of "rich" folk is not especially made up of the richer members of the church. They are the ones who consider themselves blessed and will skimp a bit to help another less fortunate. Don't abuse your givers. But also, don't overlook their spiritual giftedness. Many times older folks are willing to sponsor a child, or maybe you can set up an "adopt a grandchild" program for this.

8. Be creative and revive or adapt something from your youth group days which may be a wonderful, "fresh idea" to your group today. Whatever happened to:

—community youth group days and inter-church activities?

—visiting local street fairs or carnivals?

—concerts in the park?
—school plays or concerts?
—parent sponsored events or meals?

9. Plan an "Increasing Your Awareness" Trip. Sometimes teenagers are insulated and isolated from the poor in the community. Such a trip can help all of your teenagers to recognize the various forms and faces of poverty. This can be done from a church bus or van, if available, or by enlisting drivers from the church. Give each teenager a notebook and pen and tell them to jot down any evidence of poverty or low income that they encounter on the trip. Suggest they take their trip in silence and just look and write.

Map out a trip of about an hour in which the teenagers will see as much evidence of poverty as possible. Drive by vacant lot playgrounds, government housing, slums, used clothing stores, food pantries, abandoned neighborhoods, soup kitchens, etc. Make sure you avoid any neighborhoods from which your teenagers may come.

Upon returning, create a "faces and forms" of poverty log using the examples that the teenagers observed. Talk about it. Ask them what they thought and felt. Help them to see through the myths that "the poor choose to live that way," and "they won't help themselves." Let the kids struggle with the issues of poverty. Compile a "Suggestions to Fight Poverty" worksheet for discussion.

10. Back to the Bible! God's Word is a fabulous source of information on the plight of the poor and how concerned God is toward those who face poverty. Both Testaments are full of references showing God's eternal concern for the poor.

Numerous verses present interesting and relevant word studies. God has a lot to say about money and how it influences our relationships with Him and others. Be creative in how this material might be developed with the youth. James 1:22 — 2:26 is always a fascinating, convicting study.

11. Role play is one of the best ways I know to get the point of poverty across with teens. Develop some situations for the kids to act out, or have them dramatize Bible stories or newspaper clippings concerning the poor. Today I read of a major corporation in our area which will soon cut 1,100 jobs. What will life be like for these families? How will it impact my church and youth ministry?

As a reality check, remind them of what life for the "have nots" is like. As they act out situations, keep pressing them to remember the things that may have been plentiful in these homes but which are now missing. Did the family have to sell the TV? The stereo? What about vacations? Church camp? How does this family feel now that it has to reduce its church tithe or offering? Did they have to trade down their car? Did they have to move?

Be careful not to model any situation so that it resembles any family in your church. However, if the lay-off or plant closing occurred in your town and put your people out of work, be direct about it. Facing the problem will be a means of expression and relief for grieving teenagers.

And look beyond your community to those in other countries. Some of your low income kids may just start feeling both blessed and rich.

Our society tends to esteem position, power, and money. Christ does not. Work to model the values of Christ in your youth ministry. If this is not intentionally done, you will likely default to the values of our society. That's when the poor and low income kids feel the need to head for the door, embarrassed and unwilling to compete with the price tag of an affluent youth program. Round them up and re-think your ministry. If you do, all of the kids will benefit from the new sensitivity.

15/ Get to Work!

My guess is that you wouldn't have bought this book if your heart wasn't already in the right place. You want to reach out to the kids who haven't always had a place within the church to call home. It's a tough job.

A Chinese philosopher once said that, "A journey of a thousand miles begins with one step." As you begin your journey, I'd like to share a few concluding thoughts.

1. Don't read this book and then choose one or two types of kids to whom you would like to reach out. It is wiser to assess your present youth group at its level of existing need and target the obvious.

As I first began my ministry, I targeted juvenile delinquents. It was successful. But, looking back, I can see now that I overlooked some kids with physical handicaps who did not participate due to my zeal for other types of kids. While the delinquent kids were exciting, the handicapped kids had been faithful members of the church family. A better plan of ministry would have been to invest balanced effort to all of the kids.

Working to respond to the existing needs of the group also recognizes that the majority of kids have no severely limiting special-life situation which excludes them from participating in your youth group. In these kids you are building a foundation of acceptance and ministry that will last them a lifetime. You are also giving them steppingstones to be peer counselors. Remember, they may be the only "Bible" some others see.

With Jesus as our Model, we remember that He accepted all as they came to Him. Not an easy task, but a fulfilling one.

2. Remember the concept of the *Long Run*. Ideally, you'll be working with your kids for some time. Spread your ministry over each day that the Lord gives you with them. Don't work for the *Big Splash*. It's usually a belly flop! Rather, work toward giving them a confidence that love and ministry will be forthcoming for a good, long time.

An additional component to the wisdom of the Long Run is found in reminding ourselves that the burn-out factor in youth work is very high. To try too much at one time could be the kiss of death. Burn-out can be effectively reduced by concentrating on the Long Run.

3. I originally came up with over 30 different kinds of needy kids and special-life situations when I jotted down my thoughts for this book. Using the general principles of the opening chapters, you can work to seek out kids who were not covered. Like whom? What about the drop-out, the stuttering teen, those with emotional problems, the mentally ill, the mentally handicapped, the painfully shy, the preacher's kids, the terminally ill, the kids whose families move often. The list could go on and on.

Each type of kid has some aspect of his or her life which makes participating in a youth group unlikely. Yet, inside, I have found that these kids long for just what you are offering when your youth group meets. Assume that they want to be with you and can't quite figure out how to "break in."

Finally, reflect upon Psalm 127:1 which reminds us that, "Unless the Lord builds the house, its builders labor in vain."

Who is building the work which you lead? If it is anyone other than God, it will not stand. The temptation is great for us in youth work. The kids can give us a lot of "ego fodder" as psychologists call it when we receive the adoration of others. The test is how well the group will stand without you. If it is healthy, the group will survive beyond your ministry with them.

Let God do the building! Be honored to be His worker! Be open to each acre of the harvest field.

I wish I could know each of you reading this book. I wish I could follow your progress as you make a difference one teenager at a time. I am excited about what you will accomplish for God. Any difference is a big difference...an eternal difference.

Thank you for being willing to look beyond the comfortable and predictable. You enter new and exciting waters when you seek to minister to kids who don't fit. What a wondrous adventure lies ahead of you!

And now may the God of peace strengthen your arms to reach out and your heart to love those young people who have been hovering on the edges of your ministry, longing to become kids who do fit.

Amen!